Let's Take A Journey

Inside Nature's Mystical World

By

Lloyd W. Alexander

Contents

Preface

I would like to thank you for choosing my book. Your support of local artists and authors, such as myself, is truly appreciated. Your choice keeps the journey alive for local talent.

My journey began back in 1995 when I sold my first photograph of Portland Head Light. I had taken it after a snowstorm had recently passed. Many copies sold over the years and I have finally retired it. Since that first sale, much has changed in the world of photography, as well as in my own personal world. It has all led me to where I am now, and through those adventures, I discovered a gift for being as one with nature and wildlife.

First, I think it is important that you know that I grew up in Portland's West End. I lived there until my late thirties and had never ventured into the woods or even hiked. I was into sports and was very active, so a transition to hiking was not a stretch in general. The woods were a place that were scary to me and walking down the city streets late at night seemed a safer thing to do in my mind. I was extremely comfortable with my surroundings of steel and concrete as it was all I knew. Then it all changed.

I was diagnosed with diabetes in my early thirties and that soon set off an anxiety that gripped me, changing my world forever. I left my job at an ice arena thus starting the shrinking of my world. I hardly left my house for over two years. My world became increasingly small and I hardly spoke to anyone except for my wife. My circle of friends disappeared as I became more reclusive. Photography did not play a role in my life any longer and depression set in. Then I read an article that began a change for the better.

One day I read about geocaching and the thought of a treasure hunt intrigued me. How cool to be able to use a GPS unit, enter co-ordinates that you combined with hints, and find something hidden! Inside the uncovered caches could be little trinkets to trade or maybe just a small piece of paper to sign your ID indicating that you found it. I was able to convince my wife that this could be a good thing for me, as it would help me focus my mind on something and hopefully sidetrack the anxiety. There was a geocache just down the street from my house and that seemed like a great place to start. Using my newly learned skills, I hunted and found it. Slowly, I found more and more caches and was leaving the house on a regular basis, a step outside my previous comfort zone. That led to driving out of the city, into the country, and then on to hiking trails to find geocaches. I was hooked. I was climbing mountains and setting goals. I was alive again!

The woods still tended to frighten me but I had a goal and went for it. I began to see things I had never seen before while in these new places. Nature was new to me and it astonished me with all kinds of surprises. Birds were no longer the pigeons or gulls that I had seen in the city, but had beautiful colors and songs. This was a whole new world to be explored, and for the most part, my anxiety stayed behind on my new adventures. So many things I had never seen before started to be right in front of me! Frogs, snakes, butterflies, fox, deer, moose, and even bears! Scenic views that made me feel like I needed to wipe my eyes to make sure it was all real.

Soon, just trying to explain these wonderful things to anyone seemed too vague and boring. I didn't expect their excitement to match mine, but I could not adequately describe the true beauty in words and needed another form of communication to convey my reactions to this new world. The CAMERA!!

I dug it out and dusted it off. In just those few years, my nice film camera had gone the way of the dinosaur and was not the equipment needed for a new digitalized world. Slowly, I saved and purchased a digital camera. The pictures began to bring my new life journey home with me. The excitement stayed with me and the desire to see more grew with it. Something inside was changing.

The anxiety was still full blown in the concrete and steel world that I lived in, but out in the woods, it diminished. I discovered there were endless varieties of plants, and likewise, a vast arena of different species of birds and animals. The reactions of the birds and the animals were surprising to me as they did not bolt at the sight of me. The stories that came home with me seemed unbelievable to my friends at first, until they saw the photographs I had to go along with them.

Their excitement, combined with my own, led to more and more adventures. The stories and photographs eventually led to a few sales. The sales encouraged me to take the next step: to have a show. My friend, Becky, knew Carson, who owns a coffee shop in Gorham, ME called the Gorham Grind. Eventually, I got the courage to go speak with Carson, after an introduction from Becky. Despite never having done a show before, he gave me my first shot. The show was a huge success and now is an annual event at the Grind. I am forever grateful to Becky and Carson for giving me the opportunity to have my first show. My photography business has grown greatly from that first show, to a level beyond my wildest dreams.

I began to overcome my anxiety well enough to do more shows in various locales. I added craft shows and eventually started selling my photography in stores year round. As I write this, there are now over twenty stores displaying my photographs. I have now done solo shows where I am the featured artist at event halls, restaurants, and other wonderful venues. I have even shared my first educational presentation and told stories of my close encounters with wildlife to an audience eager to learn. I am also developing a program to educate children, to help put them in touch with the nature that awaits them right outside their door, in hopes of providing a spark to ignite a passion as the future stewards of our world. The anxiety still lurks in the shadows, but does not follow me into the wilderness any longer.

This book is my chance to take you on some of the journeys with me. In the book are stories with pictures illustrating my discovery of how I found my gift to connect with nature. I also share ways for you to learn to connect with nature as well. I want you to feel the excitement and see the beauty with your own eyes. I am not an expert; I merely share with you what I have learned by trial and error. So please seek additional information on basic hiking skills and about the area you will be hiking before setting out on your own adventures.

My experiences with wildlife have led some to call me "Dr. Doolittle" or "Grizzly Adams" and I am humbled by those kind words. I cannot explain the experiences I have with wildlife other than to say I was given a gift. I am allowed to be with nature in a truly unique way; one that often does not seem logical in how I am accepted by wildlife and how it interacts with me. My experiences seem to defy common sense in many cases, but this has allowed me to observe and learn.

I share it all with you in the pages ahead. My journey continues, and yours is about to begin!

Doolittle by a Hare?

So let us have a little fun here and a little fun there with this "Dr. Doolittle" moniker that has been placed upon me as a nickname of sorts. A little term that was used at first by a friend named Angel, and then, over time, spread to others as a way to explain what seemed, well, inexplicable. To me, it was just some interesting occurrences that happened here and there at first, but gradually these occurrences increased over time. I began to wonder if there was something to this, or was it just chance? It seemed that certain animals and I were on the same wave length. I certainly was not sure, but I did know that I was enjoying every moment of every encounter.

To ask a duck to come closer from afar and watch it as it swims to you, or to summon a goose not even seen that day and suddenly it too appears! Chance, or perhaps something else? Deer that walk from over a hundred yards away to within mere feet just to look you up and down before turning around. Seeing numerous fawns close up in one day after never being able to photograph wild ones before. Going eyeball to eyeball with a Snowy Owl. Sitting with a pair of fox trying to decide who gets to take the nap. Lounging in the woods amongst

1

some ten or more deer as the fawns walk cautiously around you. Following a young Red-tailed Hawk hunt as it swoops from tree to tree and watching it make its attempts. Getting to see a bear that was an hour's drive away, knowing it would wait until you got there.

Chance....luck.........who knows...........stories you will soon read to decide for yourself.

On one of the many weekends spent in the North Woods of NH, a remarkable event came about. I rented a canoe for my fellow photographer and friend, Naomi, and I to use. We wanted to get some images of moose and other wildlife out on the river. I had wanted to see a Snowshoe Hare and knew one of our mutual friends had a pair living under their shed, but it was over an hour away. I had rented a canoe and needed to make the most of it. After some deliberation, we decided to stay in the area we were in. I asked the guide who rented us the canoe if he had any tips on where one may find a rabbit in the general area. He explained it was not possible to see one or get any kind of pictures without his Beagles finding them, flushing them, and chasing them towards you. I smiled and thanked him anyway. As Naomi and I left, we knew that it was possible to spot a hare in the area, as I had found one in the woods near Umbagog which was not far from where we rented the canoe.

We reflected back on the one we had seen near Umbagog not long ago, as winter turned to spring, and what an amazing experience that was for us. We were walking a trail that was likely a snowmobile trail in the midst of winter, but was nothing more than a muddy wood strewn trail in the spring.

We carefully picked our way along the trail and were seeing signs of moose and bear among other things. There were several tracks that went in both directions; some old and some new. We were amazed at the number of tracks we were seeing. It had put us on a heightened sense as we expected to see or hear something on the trail at any second.

As we moved further, we saw a site where something had been killed. There was only blood and hair everywhere. We looked around to see if we could tell where something had been dragged off but didn't notice anything obvious. It didn't seem like it had been more than a day or two old. We tried to figure out what it was and finally decided to move on, as we were stumped, but had narrowed it down to a small animal like a hare.

As we walked I had drifted a bit further ahead of Naomi. I stopped to wait for her and felt like there were eyes on me. I have had this feeling before and learned that it almost always means there actually is something watching me. I slowly moved my eyes to see if I could find anything right near me. The hair on the back of my neck was not standing up and I felt no fear.

The first scan revealed nothing, and yet I knew I was looking in the right direction and that SOMETHING was there. Naomi was still slowly making her way down the trail and was still about twenty yards away. I scanned slower and blocked out every shape I knew until I came across a shape that just didn't look quite right. I stared at it and studied the shape for what seemed like forever.

Slowly the shape transformed from a brown and white mound into a Snowshoe Hare that was sitting perfectly still just off the trail and blending in with its surroundings extremely well. It was caught in the stage between winter fur and summer fur, as it was a mixture of brown and white. In the winter they are completely white and in the summer they are brown.

Spring and fall are tough times of year for them as they are going through a fur transition and are easier to spot by predators. The hare is disguised very well to blend in during the winter, as its white fur matches the snow well. During the summer, its light brown fur matches the grasses and

understory of the forest very well, as you can see in the picture to the left. But in spring and fall, especially with early melting snow in spring or an early snow in the fall, the mixture of fur colors leaves them without that perfect place to blend into their surroundings.

It was looking right back at me and seemed positive I could not see it. It is likely that I only could because it was in the middle of its change of fur between the seasons, but I also feel as though Mother Nature wanted me to see this beautiful hare in its current state to share with others.

I slowly raised the camera and snapped a few shots. I turned to Naomi, who was closer now, and was pointing to her that there was something right in front of me. She strained to pick it out just as I did, and then a smile came across her face. She began to raise her camera and snapped a few pictures. We looked at each other again and smiled.

I turned back towards the hare and it was gone, simply gone, without a noise or a trace of direction. It was simply amazing that it could disappear so quickly and effectively. Nature is astonishing in how it hides and moves.

I turned to Naomi and she shook her head, as she did not get a clear shot of the hare and also had not seen or heard it leave. We talked and enjoyed the moment. We were truly captivated by the beauty and the way something could be so well hidden, yet be right there in front of you.

After that experience, it seemed much easier for me to see Snowshoe Hare. My eyes had been opened to a new shape. My mind seemed to be able to catalogue and remember the new shapes of animals as I saw them. Each time, they would be easier to spot as they now stood out in my mind from their surroundings.

We laughed about how sly the hare had been and how neither of us even heard it leave. The memory of that encounter was fun to revisit, but we were now approaching Pontook Dam and soon the sun would set for the day.

We decided a bathroom break was in order before we put the canoe in to catch the sunset from the river. We stopped at Pontook Dam and used the restrooms. I came out first, and low and behold, a Snowshoe Hare in summer brown was out in front of the car eating grass. I paused, smiled, and immediately thanked Mother Nature for this treat. I slowly moved to the car and the rabbit turned to face me. I was thinking it would bolt now and I would just have a story to tell Naomi, and an unlikely one at that. However, the hare watched carefully but continued to graze. I opened the car door, grabbed my camera equipment, and slowly began to take images. The Snowshoe Hare moved around a bit and I was able to see it hop, pause, eat, and hop some more. I never realized just how long their bodies were when all stretched out, but this one gave me a few good looks at its seemingly endless body. Amazing, was all I could think as I watched and snapped

away. I heard Naomi come out of the restroom so I turned and motioned for her to come on down. She often just waits and lets me get the images if I am on to something. She made her way down and the rabbit took notice of her, but continued as it had before. She then raised her camera and off into the woods it went, as quick as a lightning bolt hitting the ground. She looked at me with a big smile and said "Unbelievable…only YOU could talk about wanting to see a hare, and then in fact see one two miles down the road. Unbelievable!" I yelled a thank you to the rabbit and then off we went to put the canoe in the spot we had selected. We passed the guide's house and we recalled the conversation with him earlier in the day. It gave us a good chuckle, as Mother Nature had blessed us with a beautiful hare, moments after reminiscing about the one we had seen mere months ago.

I must say that every encounter is not quite so quick to occur, and many happen out of the blue with me not wishing for anything. I go out each day prepared to see what I see and to be happy with the experiences that I will have during each day. Mother Nature always seems to have surprises for me, and sometimes, while she's giving, she also teaches me a valuable lesson or two along the way. Often, these lessons are ones our parents have repeatedly talked about as we were growing up but we just didn't take them to heart. Out in the wilderness, I have found these lessons often come back to me in a way that I truly understand them now. In a later chapter, *Fawntastic*, you will see how Mother Nature teaches me a lesson that I already knew, but once again, needed to be reminded of.

I think that I am given gifts from Mother Nature and that I am supposed to take what I am given and share this with others through photography. Mother Nature has wanted me to see that each of her gifts is as beautiful as the next. I believe the animals coming close and interacting is something I am given so that I can pass it along with true heartfelt stories or images that seem to take you into their world. I feel truly blessed to be able to share the things I see through stories and images. I am thankful for the kind words many of you have shared with me about the images. I am just a vessel through which we all are allowed to see a world that is still full of beauty and life; a world that is beyond our cell phones and iPads if we only lift our heads long enough to see it. So whether I am a little bit like "Dr. Doolittle" or not is fine with me, as long as the gifts I am given open other's eyes once in awhile to something that is right here with us and so very beautiful. My journey........is your journey.....I hope you continue to come along and look through my lens into the beauty of Nature.

Dark and Scary

The woods can seem so big that it is often overwhelming to many, and it can be a downright scary place to be with many unfamiliar noises and dark shadowy places seemingly everywhere. Add that to the fact that the further you walk, the further you are from other people, and help in general. Fears can grow in an instant and the search to calm those fears can take quite a while. The woods used to be that way for me.

The place I felt comfortable was in the city streets. I grew up in Portland, ME, and while not the largest city in the world, it was still one that had crime, dark alleys, and unpredictable areas where sometimes you were welcomed by the neighborhood kids and others when you simply were not. It was the way of the city and just something I knew as my life. Walking an alley late at night certainly would put you on alert, but you felt secure in that you would hear or sense something before it happened. Instincts deep within you would kick in with fight or flight ready to go. Yet it was not a fear that I felt, as this was home to me.

I personally never had trouble in the city and consider myself fortunate for that. Many friends had encounters and some ended up injured or robbed over the years. This was typical of city life and was expected, if not accepted. The concrete and steel that surrounded us was our forest and one we knew well. The sounds, smells, and sights were something we could interpret easily and quickly. We had adapted to a different way of life than our ancestors who, only generations before, would have experienced a rougher and wilder existence closer to the forest.

Yet to many who live in the city, the thoughts of a walk in the forest bring many questions to mind, and for me it brought a sense of uneasiness. I did not know anything about the forest or the wildlife within it. It was a complete mystery to me and one that seemed to be shrouded in an impenetrable fog. Even the parks in the city that had large areas of trees were foreign to me. I would visit and simply could not understand what I was hearing or seeing. The sounds meant nothing and often my mind would conjure up something I should fear and keep me on alert. So I did not visit these places often. Then it just suddenly began to change and the catalyst for that was geocaching.

Geocaching is a game of sorts; I guess you would say it could be an adult form of hide-n-seek, except it is not people who you seek but something hidden. You use clues and a Global Positioning System (GPS) unit to help guide you to the right place and then you will find the treasure. Some "treasures" are big like old army ammunition boxes and others can be very tiny. You find them and can take anything you want from the box, but also must leave something new in return. You also sign your name to let others know you found it. I had issues with anxiety disorder that kept me home bound for a few years.

Geocaching became a portal out of the house. I found as many caches as I could near my home in Portland, but soon had to move further and further to find new caches. The anxiety eventually led me away from populated areas and to the mountains and forests. A dream had always been to climb Mount Washington and the mountains surrounding it. I had seen those mountains so many times from Portland's Western Promenade and dreamed of a mysterious and wonderful place on those snow covered peaks. It was a dream, and one I doubted I would ever realize as I had never climbed anything except the hills in Portland. Soon geocaching made the dream seem in the realm of possibilities, but only if I could get over the mountains of anxiety that were now my dark and scary forest.

On my first hike to find a cache on a mountain, I faced many obstacles which were simply creations of my own mind. I believe those to be the worst kind of obstacles, as you can't grab them but they can certainly grab you. My first mountain was Burnt Meadow in Western Maine and it proved to be a challenge for me in many ways. I read about the mountain and the trail as much as I could to try and prepare for it. However, it is nearly impossible to wrap your mind around the unknown and anxiety has a way of finding and amplifying those things even further. I was in for a challenge.

I remember sitting in my car in the parking lot for a while before finally convincing myself the first steps would be the hardest and each would get easier after that. It certainly seemed to be logical that after I started, it would get easier, but that proved to be wrong on this venture into the unknown. Each step brought me deeper into the fears and each step brought me further from where I thought I needed to be; back in my car, headed home, on my way back towards the city. Yet

I fought on, taking step after step up the trail. Sometimes these steps were very slow and other times very fast. I could feel, hear, and maybe even see my heart beating. I was in shape, so it was not from physical exertion that I was all amped up. It was not excitement. It was certainly fear! To try to calm myself I would stop and just listen and listen. The problem wasn't that I couldn't hear anything, as I had assumed the woods would likely be a fairly quiet place to be most of the time; the problem was, I COULD hear so many things and I simply could not sort them out to be anything I could identify. All I heard were sounds; sounds which were so foreign to me.

That, of course, left my mind to devise its very own source for the sounds and often the ominous meaning it had with it. Fear grew, steps became harder to take, and self-doubt began to rise with each moment. What was I doing and what was I thinking? I stood still for at least five minutes and just tried to pick apart the wave of sounds before me, but truly struggled to discern one from another. I decided I either needed to move forward or turn and leave. I knew though if I left, the fear would only grow, and whatever was out there would only become worse in my mind. What was the worst that could happen? I did not know, but I was sure fearful of running into a bear. A nightmare of a scenario began to play in my head as the sounds still danced undefined around me: a chorus of natural sounds, a chorus of taunts, or a chorus of warnings?

Time to move forward and that is just what I'd do on that day on Burnt Meadow Mountain. I followed the path and the GPS unit until I was on top of the mountain and found the cache. Success, or so it seemed at the moment. The fear quickly returned and reminded me I still needed to hike down the mountain, but now it was later in the day, the sun was behind the mountain and it was getting darker in the woods. I could not stay on the mountain, so I slowly headed back down, stopping often to listen to the sounds as I did not want to surprise anything. I would scuff my feet to make some noise and even tried to whistle, but when I could not hear the sounds over my whistling I quickly stopped. Senses remained on high alert even after I made it back to the car and pulled out of the parking lot. Driving home my nerves began to calm and I replayed the trip in my head, but the answers I was looking for were not there for me. There were just sounds and feelings that I was not sure how to overcome.

It became evident I needed to learn more about what was out there in the woods and how it would likely behave. I needed to know the common sounds and signs of animals, as well as the common sounds of a forest or I would quickly become too anxious, too afraid of the unknown, and any dreams of being free in the woods or climbing Mount Washington would fade forever.

There was no book to help someone to learn sounds but there were books on animals, trees, birds, and other things available to educate me. There were books on hiking safely and hiking etiquette. I read them all and continue to read anything I can find even now.

The woods are dark and certainly can be scary, but you can learn how to face your own fears and battle your own mind. Arming yourself with knowledge and pushing forward will be easier. Develop the skill to hear sounds and know what they are, and learn to observe your surroundings to better understand them. Humans are logical, and if we can make sense of sounds and sights in the woods, then we can calm ourselves. If we leave it as unknown, then the fear will creep in and begin to overtake rational thoughts.

Things changed for me over time and I now find the greatest peace in the woods and have come to love the sounds. I understand more of them than I ever dreamed possible and my knowledge continues to grow. I can distinguish different sounds made by a leaf being rustled and know why it moved. That has taken time, but I have swapped lifelong comfort in a city full of shadows and dark alleys for a new level of comfort in those deep, dark, and scary woods. Now I hike the forest paths and I do not like to walk the streets. The sounds and behavior of wildlife in the forest can be more predictable than the unpredictable people on the city streets.

I will walk you through many of the techniques I use to feel comfortable in a place that was once so foreign but has now come to symbolize a place of peace and serenity. I can only hope you are able to find a little part of it after reading this book. I hope you enjoy the stories of my encounters with wildlife as I share what I have learned about the animals and their habitats. So let us continue to take this journey together...

The Calling

Nature is something I love to share with others and sometimes special moments happen during these sharing times. They are the most unexpected, but also the most fun, as the gift I have been given is then visible to others. It also results in an intimate experience for them with wildlife that they would never have had. I never know why it happens and I truly can't explain why it occurs in some instances and not in others.

I truly believe that wildlife can sense a person's intent and pick up on subtle things such as nervousness as well. They know if your heart is pure and you will not harm them. They seem to sense many things beyond what you would think they are capable of and what they are given credit for. This day was one that showed a greater sense of communication than is logically possible.

I give photography lessons, and on this particular day, I was working with a friend who wanted a lesson. We stopped at a few different locations looking for wildlife before ending up in Westbrook along the Presumpscot River. This is a great place in the winter months and early spring to get photos of ducks that range from the truly rare to those that you normally do not get to see because they are in a different habitat the majority of the year. For the photography lesson, there is always a large group of mallards and gulls on hand, and ready to be the subject for the tutorial.

We made our way around and were taking images here and there, as I showed Angel different techniques to photograph birds flying or moving about and talking about

what to expect and how to predict some of the likely movements these birds make. If you can learn to predict or anticipate a little, then it helps you to be ready for a shot. As we walked, I noticed an American Coot on the far side of the river. This would be a bird you rarely see except in a location such as this in the winter. There was excitement for me as I told Angel about the bird.

She had never seen one before, so I told her I would try to get it to come over and see us, but it didn't always work. She looked at me funny even though she had heard stories of other things that had happened with me and wildlife. I took a moment to clear my mind and settle into the peaceful place that I am in when I am in the wild. Then I vocally asked the coot to come on over close, so Angel could see him and we could take some pictures of it. Mere moments later, the coot turned in our direction and began to swim towards us.

Angel just looked at me and then said, "Unbelievable! I can't believe it is really coming over here." I smiled as the coot kept coming until it was in front of us and just offshore. I thanked it for coming and we began to take some shots. After it had been with us for about five minutes, I again thanked it and told it we were done if it needed to move on. One last glance our way and then it swam on its way.

Angel had a large smile on her face and said, "That was amazing. How do you do that?" I explained that I truly did not know and that it did not work every time that I asked either. I think it has to do with many variables which I just do not fully understand. I know that when I have a clear mind, the animals seem less threatened and more receptive to interaction with me. That is part of the magical experience between the wildlife and I.

I told her I would try it again, just to show her it was not a fluke. I felt like everything was aligned for it to work today. I felt like I was at the right place in my mind to communicate with the birds. I explained to her that there was always a domestic goose in the area and it hung out with a Canada Goose that had a broken wing. They would be there somewhere, but we had not seen nor heard them. She agreed that we had not and said there was no way I could get them here. I smiled and then vocally asked them to come to where we were in the next five minutes so Angel could meet them.

In just a couple minutes, they came around the corner and began to call out as they approached us on the bank. Angel's mouth dropped open and then she said, "Oh my God, I can't

believe this....amazing!" They stopped in front of us and I thanked them as we took a few pictures. Soon they were on their way and we continued finding things to photograph as the lesson continued

I rarely ask wildlife to come to me as I tend to just let them be as they wish to be and let them decide if they want to interact with me. It is their choice and I am always happy either way. However, there are times when it is something I have not seen before or would just like to get a better look at. I do not always ask vocally either. Sometimes, I may just wish for it to linger a bit longer where it is so I can take a couple more shots or simply observe it. Other times I may let it know I truly mean it no harm or that I am going to move away so it can stay where it is and do what it wishes. I truly can't explain how or why this happens. There often seems to be no rhyme or reason for it.

I truly appreciate the fact that it does happen and feel blessed by it. Something so very illogical and so very beautiful, yet seemingly so hard to believe; so real, it makes me tingle each time it happens. A true gift given to me…it feels surreal and I appreciate it.

Walking in the Woods

A stroll, a walk, or even a hike can sound like such an easy thing to do and brings forth images of a peaceful trail with trees overhanging, birds chirping, and the smell of pine as you meander along. You choose the pace you wish to pass the time. So simple and so peaceful, and so tried and true as well, but yet missing so much along the way. This is how I used to walk in the woods until I began to understand that I was missing so much around me. I needed to change the way I walked in the woods.

One day, when I was sitting on a stump just off Crawford Path in Crawford Notch in the White Mountains of New Hampshire, I was awakened to new sounds and movement that at first startled me. I turned at the rustling leaves behind me, as there seemed to be a growing disturbance. As I spun around I saw a shape dart off. I had apparently scared whatever it was as much as it had startled me. I sat and stared but could not find it in the thicket that lay just a bit further off the trail. My mind began to race and to imagine so many different things. I wanted to get up and leave, but I was also curious as to what it might have been. I wondered if I remained quiet, would return from the shadows? The unknown evokes a reaction in all of us and for me it was a mix of fear and excitement. I decided to just sit still.

The woods, which were silent after my sudden movement, began to come back to life about ten minutes later. I truly felt as if it was an eternity as I stared into the thicket in anticipation. At first, chickadees began to tweet and flutter around me, then a rustle off to the side of me from a Red Squirrel, scolding me with a bark, as my presence was not welcome in his area of the forest. Other common sounds began to come into focus as my mind opened to what was around me in a way it had not done before. I could hear the wind pass through the leaves and the gentle trickling of the stream running down the mountain. There was life here that I had inadvertently ignored.

A leaf moved before my eyes and a snake poked its head out from under it. A simple Garter Snake lending its beauty to the scene that was evolving before me, seemingly as each second passed. A scene I had found so simple when I first sat down had evolved into a complex view of life in the woods. Every step I had taken on all paths were now passing before my eyes as I tried to see what I had missed. So much that happens here in this little window of life that easily goes unnoticed.

Movement in the thicket snaps me back to the present and refocuses me on what could be in there. I see a dark blob moving about and I try to match what I see with known shapes in my mind, but nothing is linking up to tell me what this is that stays hidden. I remain still and the bushes move. The sound is almost deafening now that I am zeroed in on it. I can now make out some red on the head, but is it a bird or an animal? My mind races for answers as fear begins to swell from my inner depths and my body prepares for fight or flight.

Slowly it begins to reveal itself. A beautiful male Spruce Grouse is now in the open before me and looking right at me. Slowly, it proudly makes its way towards where I am sitting. A beautiful red crown appears on its head and white streaking across its bold chest which is puffed as it continues forward. Does it see me? I think that it simply must, and sure enough, it gives a low krrrk, krrrk, krrrk in my general direction. It keeps coming until it is some five feet away and there it continues to make its low vocal calls. I am now looking at the grouse eye to eye as it continues its call. I sit in awe of the beauty of what was just hidden from my sight moments ago. The Red Squirrel no longer protests my presence and comes down towards the grouse. Off goes the grouse and the squirrel takes over. I watch for a moment as the squirrel recovers the cone it must have dropped when I was approaching. The cone secured, the squirrel scurries off and I decide to walk some more.

This day was one that changed my idea of walking in the woods, and time and again, it has proven to be a lesson that I am grateful to have stumbled upon. Walking in the woods can be very simple or it can be our chance to look deeper and to be part of a world that has much more to offer than we could ever imagine. How can you walk and be aware of things? How can you walk and remain safe from the things you do not wish to see?

Observation will need to become a key to getting in tune with your surroundings. The ability to let your mind find peace and settle on the world around you is something you will need to learn as well. It is not an easy thing to do, as our world is so fast paced now and the demands on our time seem to follow us everywhere. So lessen that commotion by turning off your cell phone and anything else that could be distracting. Before you even begin to walk the trail, pause at the start of it and simply close your eyes. Count slowly to ten and then listen to the sounds around you. Identify the ones you can until you are left with the ones you simply can't figure out. It may take you awhile the first time, as there will be many you do not recognize. Open your eyes and see if you can locate the ones you could identify. Then try closing your eyes again and imagine their locations around you. Ah, an image now forms in your mind and you can place things around you. Slowly tune out the ones you know and listen for those that you do not know. Try to place them in the image of the world you have and the sounds you know. Concentrate on just one and listen to it to see if it changes or is a constant. You can now narrow down where it is coming from, so open your eyes and see if you can find it. Try this for some of the other new sounds. You are learning to observe with not only your eyes but with your ears as well.

Move along the trail now and walk as little or as far as you want, but stop from time to time and just listen. Practice the listening and the looking at each stop. When you take the time to rest or have lunch, try doing the same thing. Try to do it with other people around. It is good to learn to be able to block out the sounds you know, to hear and get used to the ones you do not. In time, many sounds will be added to what you know and the world you see and hear around you in the woods will grow immensely.

How can you combine these new observations through sounds to help you see things that you may not normally see because they disappear before you are ever close enough to view them?

A key to this next step is adapting to the ground that is below your feet. Every trail has different terrain and finding a way to walk quietly on it is very important. The stealthier you are, the better the chance you will have to get closer to the animals. It is also important that you understand that being stealthy may also put you in the possible position of a confrontation with an animal such as a bear or a moose which can be extremely dangerous. Always keep this in mind, as you can alter your approach by being just a bit louder or more cautious. An animal that hears you coming is likely to simply run away before you are too close.

Types of terrain can be anywhere from loose rocks or gravel, to fallen leaves, to frozen ground or ice in the winter. It will take you a few steps to find the spot that is the quietest and that may change throughout the trail. Keep an eye out for things that will cause a loud noise, such as twigs or branches, that you could step on and snap. Also, watch out for rocks that can be kicked or anything you can move with your feet that will make a louder noise. I generally move on the side of the trail but do not venture off the trail, as it is easy to damage precious vegetation. In fact, some vegetation in the Alpine Zone can be destroyed forever by one single foot step. The Alpine Zone is a natural region or biome that does not contain trees because it is at a high altitude. The Presidential Range of the White Mountains contains many places with this unique zone. I also stay on the inside edge of the trail while traveling around a curve. This means I can't see too far down the trail and I can't see around the corners which offer its own risks and rewards.

Approaching a corner in a trail requires you to slow down, keep your eyes open, and truly use your ears and listen for movement. If you hear any sounds of movement, you should try to lower your profile to keep out of sight of anything approaching from down the trail. Listen for a little while to see what the sound possibly could be and then you can decide to do one of the following: move forward, move backward or continue observing. If it is an animal you are hoping to see, then it is time to let it settle back down; be patient as it may have heard you move. Once it settles, slowly ease your way forward, a few steps at a time, with a low profile around the corner. Stay close to cover and eventually you will be able to see what it is, and if you do it right, you can get photographs of it before it even knows you are looking at it. Again, remember, if this is a bear, be very careful and be on the lookout for cubs. If you see cubs you need to back away and not take chances of getting too close, as getting between a mom and her babies can be deadly. This is a good rule of thumb to follow for most of the larger animals (bear, moose…). Respect for animals and their space are keys to being safe, both for you and for the animal.

Another place you may happen upon is a crossing of a trail where two or more trails merge. Stop and stay on the trail you are on. Concentrate on what you hear and then slowly peak out to look down each trail. Animals will use the trails too, as it is easier than walking through the woods or brush. You will also, at some point, come across a game trail. A game trail is different than a human hiking trail and can be distinguished by the small width of the trail and the look of compacted vegetation and/or mud. These game trails generally intersect a road or hiking trail and lead deeper into forested areas. Even game trails that moose use would not leave a wide trail like the hiking trails we use to go through forests or up mountains. You can follow these, but the risks increase. Look for recent use of the game trail and remain on the regular trail in a spot to observe the game trail. Recent use could be freshly broken twigs or branches, fresh tracks or scat. These are easier to see in mud or snow, but can be seen in all conditions. Techniques on tracking and tracks can be found online at various sites or in various books. You do not need to be an expert in this area, but knowing the scat or print of some of the animals you hope to see will be helpful. Researching and acquiring knowledge over time about what animals are in each type of habitat will also assist with identification of animal signs such as tracks and scat, but for now, be excited that you have found evidence of life that you may have overlooked in the past. In time, as you spend more time in the woods, you will begin to associate different animals and their signs in certain types of surroundings/habitats.

Walking in the woods can be a fun and great adventure. Take the time to learn the sounds and you will be greatly ahead of where you are today. Learn to be patient and observe what is around you. The woods are alive, and you can see that life by changing your general approach to being in the woods. Just remember, it will take time and luck to get to a point where these things come naturally and the sighting of wildlife begins to happen more frequently. Though difficult at times, no animal or bird is impossible to see during the day, so keep your mind open and enjoy the experiences. Learning to appreciate what you have seen and being open to what is there, rather than having expectations and looking for only what you want to see, is key to not missing what is right in front of you. Take what is given.

I Will Be There

Sometimes, when wildlife is involved, I seem to know something that seems impossible to know, but yet it turns out to be true. One of these occasions was when a friend called me on her way to North Conway from her home in Berlin, NH.

She was driving on Route 16, which goes through Pinkham Notch. Some great attractions are on the road as it goes through the mountains. The Mount Washington Auto Road, the AMC Highland Center, several trails to Mount Washington, several trails to waterfalls, ski slopes, and a zip line are all there to be enjoyed. So many beautiful places are available on this one road in one notch.

As for wildlife, you can see moose at almost any time on the road and plenty of birds as well. I have seen deer eating apples near the Ranger Station. I had never seen a bear there though and had not heard of anyone else who had seen one there either. However, they are known to be in the area.

Naomi called me as she neared Storyland which is just beyond the notch area and almost back into North Conway.

Cell service in the middle part of the notch is spotty at best. She stated I would never guess what she had just seen but I sure tried to. Moose, Bull Moose, baby moose, owl, crossbills, and on I went till I was pretty sure she must have seen an alien as I had guessed everything else. She laughed, and as she began to tell me it struck me smack dab in the forehead, a BEAR! I truly have a fascination with bears and believe their spirit is a very strong one. I fear them and yet love them. They make me nervous and yet calm. I really have trouble wrapping my mind around it all.

She told me it was across from the parking lot of the Mount Washington Auto Road, eating blueberries and drawing quite a crowd. Well, the bear certainly was trying to fatten up for the winter, but the crowd does not bode well for it lingering around long. Yet something in my heart and mind told me it would wait for me.

I relay this to Naomi and she is surprised that under the circumstances, I am going to drive about one and a half hours to try and see this bear. I told her I know it may sound crazy, but I said it would wait and it would give me five minutes when I got there before it left. Naomi answered, "Only you could believe that, but I think you're crazy"! I probably was off my rocker to drive that far under the circumstances, but I could feel it in my soul and knew it would be there.

I hopped in the car and headed out. A few times the reasonable side of my brain tried to change my mind and get me to turn the car around. Yet my heart led me onward, as I just knew it would be there. It was truly illogical to think it would be, and yet, I knew it would be.

Onward I drove, and as I passed Storyland, and I felt a surge of excitement come over me. Onward still, and as I passed the AMC Highland Center, I just knew it was still there. I continued down from the ski area towards my final destination. I could see cars, motorcycles, and trucks on both sides of the road. I pulled over and parked the car. I grabbed my cameras and headed towards the crowd.

A small opening allowed me through, and there was the bear not fifty yards away, munching on blueberries. It paused and then stood up to look around. I felt like it knew I was there. Our eyes seemed to meet and it settled back to the ground. I snapped away and tried to get many different angles of the bear. It was a good sized Black Bear and very healthy looking too. As I continued to snap, a discomfort and uneasiness overcame me.

It began to envelop me and as I watched the bear. I began to realize why I was having this feeling.

I stepped back into the crowd and behind it. I had taken enough pictures of the bear. I would have loved more, but not in this situation. I could sense the bear was becoming anxious, as the people had formed a half circle around it. Some continued to get closer and closer. The bear was no longer eating blueberries, which nobody in the crowd seemed to notice. It sat up, scanned the crowd and then looked at the bank behind it. The only way the people have left it to exit is down a steep embankment and across a stream. The bear stood and seemed to be searching, so I stood taller, hoping it would see me. I kept thinking: be calm, you are ok, go down to the stream...go...go...go.

Our eyes met and it felt like there was a connection made between us. The bear dropped to all fours and ran for the embankment to escape. Amazingly, some people followed it towards the embankment, snapping away with their cameras. I could feel the bear's fear as it lunged into the water and bound away into the forest. I stood there, stunned, as people filtered back to their cars, some talking about how exciting that was and that they were truly exhilarated.

I can't help but think that this could have turned out so very different. If the bear had run anywhere but where it did, then someone likely would have been knocked down at the very least. They had not left the bear many options to escape and certainly were invading its boundaries. If the bear had somehow injured someone, then it is the bear that would have paid the price. It would likely have been put down because it hurt a human, despite the fact the humans brought it on. No thought was given to the bear's needs or safety during that whole time, as people just got caught up in being so close to a bear. The excitement is certainly understandable, but since we see ourselves as stewards of this world, we must have a greater respect for the creatures in it.

Please be careful and think of the animal. Enjoy the view, but at a distance that is safe for the both of you.

The bear waited for me and I got my five minutes with the bear. I truly enjoyed seeing the bear, but at the same time, it was a troubling experience as well. Naomi was only a little surprised it waited, as she has seen some of the other gifts given to me by Nature. In this case, maybe it was meant for me to urge the bear to go in the direction it went. That doesn't seem logical, but yet, when I made eye contact, that made perfect sense.

Update: In the summer of 2012, I met up with this bear again. It was in a field happily eating blueberries. I sat on the edge of the field and our eyes met again, with the bear looking much more at peace. I was able to sense that it was ok for me to sit there and take pictures. I could tell it was my friend by its distinguishing left ear, which had been damaged. I think it was good for both of our souls to meet again under these favorable conditions where we could both just simply enjoy, and be one with nature.

Da Dum de Dum da Whoa

The following encounter is a perfect example of using your powers of observation in the environment around you to maximize your chances of seeing wildlife. The more things you can put on your side of the board to increase your chances, the better. In this case, it was early January, and while temperatures had been around normal for that time of year, the depth of snow was minimal at best. Many lakes were barely frozen and thus streams and rivers had areas of open flowing water as well. Add to that, on this day, it had been snowing lightly. A half inch or so had fallen with more accumulating as time passed. These were advantages for me.

As I slowly started out on a snowmobile trail, the first thing I noticed was the ground, now covered with this new blanket of fresh snow, was vacant of any tracks. As I took more steps, I realized the snow was muting the noise coming from my footfalls to almost no noise at all. These two things alone certainly make it easier to see fresh tracks or fresh scat and to keep one's presence secreted. I walked on slowly and paused occasionally to listen for sounds that might give hints as to what direction I should head. I heard the bubbling water of a stream and decided to head that way.

All animals need to drink and thus areas with water such as lake shores, ponds, and streams are a great place to check anytime you come across them. In the winter, it is especially important to pay attention to open water. Water sources begin to freeze up as the winter moves along, so if you can hear water, then it is worth checking out that area for animal activity. As areas of open water shrink, so do the areas where animals can go for water. This fact should help you to pick a spot to observe wildlife in the colder part of the year.

As I began to walk towards the sound of the water, I crested a small rise and the stream was visible below, but no open water could be seen at this point. There was a bridge for the snowmobiles to cross at the bottom of gully. I stopped to listen, as approaching too quickly could result in scaring away any animal that may be near. As I surveyed the area around me, I saw tracks that were covered, thus old, but it was still a good sign.

Taking a few more cautious steps, I could see signs of fresh tracks just off to the side of the trail. I walked over to see if I could recognize them and possibly have an idea of what had been in the area. I was able to tell the tracks were made by a Snowshoe Hare and probably not long ago, as the tracks were still very clean and few flakes had fallen inside them to dull the prints. A sense of excitement surged through me as I now knew life had been here recently. I had to keep myself in check and not run down to the bridge.

I continued to slowly make my way down the rise and more prints began to appear, but now a second print was there that I did not know by a quick glance. This, of course, made me even more eager to proceed as I could possibly see something unanticipated. I continued walking down to the bridge and could finally see the open water. There was open water to the left side of the bridge about the size of a place mat and two areas on the other side that were each slightly smaller than a dinner plate. Tracks were on both sides of the bridge and led towards and way from the water. The hare tracks were joined by squirrel tracks and those mystery tracks I did not recognize. I looked for a good spot to observe both sides of the bridge without blocking access for any animals that may want to cross. I made myself comfortable and got the camera settings ready for the weather and lighting conditions; something I should have done before I even began the journey.

It was now time to use my ears and listen carefully to the world around me, listening for anything that may provide a clue of something coming towards me. In this situation, your ears become very important, however your eyes remain the most important because, with light snow on the ground, you are less likely to hear anything moving around. The gurgle of trickling water and the occasional snapping of the ice will not serve you well, so try to block those out. Use your eyes to take a slow look around and see where things are located and what areas may be the best routes for something to approach. If you are not able to discern a possible route, then still scan the area and observe your surroundings. It is important to become familiar with where you are as sometimes you may see a different shape the next time you make an observation. That new shape very well could be an animal or a bird that has come in and is now observing you or the area before coming into the open. Remember, for the wildlife, it is a life and death world. Make sure your movements are slow and try to not move your body very much. Scan with your eyes and slowly move your head. Then sit still and just observe. As it moves into view, slowly ready the camera and have fun.

As I was patiently waiting near the bridge, I detected a quick movement across from me and something was headed for one of the dinner plate sized holes. I slowly raised the camera and the animal paused. It had been moving in a "dumb da de dumb" bouncy way down to the stream until it spotted me and put on the breaks in a big "whoa" sort of way. My eyes met its beady little eyes just before the camera came to my face and my finger pushed to focus and start taking pictures. Almost as quickly, the brown ferret like animal bounded towards the hole. I snapped away and it bounced away. Each bounce seemed so slow and beautiful. Snow would fly from behind it and in front of it as each set of feet moved in and out of the fresh snow. Its body contorted like a slinky in the middle as it moved closer and closer to the hole. It seemed to take forever and yet it was over in less than two seconds, as the little animal covered the ground quickly and with ease slipped into the water.

Was it over so quickly? I decided to wait and see what would happen next, as the animal was one I did not know and wanted to see again. Also, it had gone underwater so I knew it would have to come back up somewhere. I was hoping it would be in one of the areas I could readily see and not some spot where I would not get to enjoy it again. I waited but it did not come up in any of those spots. I began to wonder how long it could stay under water when suddenly, I heard the ice under the banking across from me begin to break. Finally! This was time to pay attention to the sounds from the water and the ice! I focused on the area and soon a head popped out from under the banking but it darted back in when it spotted me. I waited with the camera ready and quickly snapped shots as the animal poked its head out three more times. It then seemed to decide it was best to stay where it was for the time being.

To me, this meant it was time to leave and let the animal do whatever it needed or wanted to do without the interference of my presence. I was blessed to have had the time and enjoyed the moment, but as I said earlier, it is life or death for the animal out here. I always try to leave as soon as I feel there is a sign of stress or that I have been there long enough, whichever comes first, as it is their home and their place. So off I went to follow other tracks and listen for other sounds.

I would find out later that the animal I had seen was an American Mink. This was a new animal for me and I was very pleased to have seen it. Such opportunities do not occur if I do not use my powers of observation to my advantage, especially when tracking animals in the snow and open water. Taking time before your journey begins to develop a plan for the conditions of the day will help you when the moment comes to capture the beauty that presents itself. It is also important to be prepared for environmental changes that may occur throughout the day, as a simple cloud overhead will change the lighting for you and may also change the movement of wildlife who adapt quickly to subtle fluctuations in their habitat. Remember, we are blessed to have such beautiful habitats and sometimes the blessings are even bigger when we are able to see some of the creatures that live there. Keep your eyes and ears open, and thankfully take what is given.

The Hawk

I have had a lot of very neat experiences with wildlife that has really opened my eyes to the fact that nature is so much more a part of everything that happens in the world than I ever used to think. I have been invited into a world that many never get to see and have had experiences that many will never have. This experience was a very special one, as this young

hawk allowed me to be a part of its search for food; the hunt.

There is a Red-tailed Hawk at Gilsland Farm in Falmouth, ME that hangs around the main Audubon building and is usually easy to find. He has been there now for a few years and is not afraid to drop down in front of people if it means he can grab something to eat, such as a squirrel or chipmunk. Children and adults have enjoyed the show as the hawk goes about its business. I have watched and photographed him since he was young.

On one occasion, I was invited to be a part of its search away from the open area of the buildings and into the woods. I had seen the hawk and said hello, which always seemed to get me a quizzical look from it, as if it was trying to understand what I was saying. I think in some ways it had an understanding that it was a greeting, and on this day, I got a low call back to which I happily replied back, asking how its day was going. We went back and forth for a couple of minutes with me talking and the hawk almost grunting. It was not a sound I normally have heard from any hawk before. It was almost as if we were having a "secret" conversation. I turned to go back to watching the other birds and taking some photographs, but the hawk kept making its little grunt and I eventually turned around. It flew to a tree about ten yards away and grunted again. I wasn't sure if I was supposed to follow, but decided I would, and it waited until I got to the tree and then began to scan the ground below. I knew it was searching for food, so decided to leave it to its hunt, but as soon as I turned to leave, it grunted again. I thought, "OK, this is weird", but I would play along and see what it wanted, if in fact, it wanted anything at all.

It flew off to another tree and landed on a low branch, watching me until I came close to it. Since I knew the hawk was hunting, I thought it would be best to try and hide so I didn't scare off whatever it may be able to find in the leaf litter below. We were both in our spots, waiting patiently.

At first I was watching the ground but realized that he would hear something and react way before I would even have a clue. So I turned my attention to watching him. He scanned the ground slowly and I could see its eyes open and then narrow. Its head would tilt slowly as it was listening to sounds I could not hear. I closed my eyes and tried to hear what it was hearing. Slowly, I was able to block out the louder sounds that I knew, and began to hear softer sounds like leaves rustling. To my ears though, it was all just rustling leaves, but to the hawk, it meant a potential source of food that may be moving leaves around. This was truly when I began to learn to listen better and to understand that sounds were not just simply sounds in nature's world. Each one had a meaning, and to creatures such as a hawk, these sounds were keys to its life. The hawk needed to know what was making the sound and if it was worth pursuing for food. A vole will make a sound, as would a chipmunk, as would a squirrel, but each is different and each has a value in the hawk's food consumption.

As humans in a developed country, we can always get food and we are often gluttonous. In the world of nature, this isn't the case, and each chance for food has to be weighed in a very different manner. Energy spent versus energy gained is part of the equation for wildlife, but it is not the only factor. If the sources for food are numerous or if the creature has eaten recently, then that factors into what it may chase after. Starving, with minimal chance for other food, anything making noise becomes valuable. But when full, and presented with multiple choices, the easiest prey is likely to get chased. This hawk would seem to be on the plenty of food part of the chain, as there are numerous chipmunks, squirrels, mice, voles, snakes, and more around Gilsland Farm. Yet this is also a young hawk that is still learning to efficiently hunt.

So it seemed that learning was part of what I was doing that day, and for the hawk, I think it was attempting to hone its skills at catching animals in different places rather than hoping to just catch them out near the feeders and the open land at the main buildings.

It could have simply been a game or a challenge to the hawk, but either way, it would benefit by doing this. In the end, it would not be in uncharted territory if food was tougher to find or if it left Gilsland Farm.

It seemed to be uninterested in anything it could see at this tree so we moved on about forty yards to another tree where, again, it picked a branch low to the ground and watched me as I walked to catch up. To see this fairly large bird fly so gracefully between limbs and branches was an awesome sight. It would nimbly turn this way or that on a course that always seemed to be destined to run it right into something. I knew they could fly through the woods, but for some reason I thought it would be at a slower pace than what I was seeing. The hawk flew as if it were out in the open fields and had no fears. I was waiting to cringe, as I expected this young hawk to graze a limb or branch and tumble to the ground. Not a chance of that happening, and in fact, it was me who stumbled as I was nearing the tree. My eyes were on the hawk and not at all watching for roots that always seem ready to grab at your feet, like this one did. I did not fall but certainly made a fair amount of noise which brought a harsh look from the hawk and a quick call before it flew off to another tree. Apparently I had messed up this spot and was getting no sympathy from my hunting partner either. I guess the reality is that in his world, second chances are rare and doing what I did was the same as missing a potential meal and going hungry. I was pretty sure I still had a PB&J in my backpack and that I would not go hungry. I was not the one to suffer a consequence for my clumsiness.

Finally, I quietly make it to the new tree. The hawk is scanning fairly fast and then I see it tilt its head and its eyes narrow. I listen carefully and can hear the sounds of leaf litter being moved around. It is louder than what I had heard earlier,

but I still had no idea what was making the noise. I saw the hawk tense and raised my camera to capture what I knew was coming any second. The hawk leapt from the tree towards the sound on the ground buried within the leaf litter. I moved at the same time to change my angle and stepped on a twig that snapped, sending a sound that seemed way too loud for what it was that I stepped on. I had made a mistake again by making noise at the most crucial of times. The hawk landed on the ground and out squirted a chipmunk from the litter. The hawk leapt towards it, but missed again, and the chance to get the chipmunk had now passed as it ducked into a hole.

The hawk stood with its legs extended and looked me in the eyes. The look said it all and if an animal can make you feel like a bumbling fool, then that is exactly how this hawk had made me feel. I had made the crucial mistake during the crucial time. I had taken a few shots and while maybe I had captured what I needed, the hawk had not. It seemed as if the moment was frozen in time as our eyes were locked: the young hawk and the bumbling, apologetic photographer. He flew back to the branch and seemed to study me with disapproving eyes before letting out a true cry and flying off into the sky high above the trees where I could not follow. A couple more cries sounded as it circled above and I began the walk back towards my car with a very lonely feeling.

As I reached the open parking lot, the hawk flew low and landed near my car. I looked at the hawk and it looked at me with the same quizzical look it normally greets me with when I say hello. This time I said goodbye and opened the car door. A quick grunt and off it flew back to the center where it could find an easier lunch.

I believe we both learned lessons that day and ones that I think will stay with both of us. For the hawk, it likely learned hunting is something to be done alone and that, while it is comfortable around humans, it is not the same as us and we are not the same as it. Quiet to us and quiet to it mean two different things.

I was able to learn how to listen better and how to begin to distinguish sounds. I learned just how important that was in the hawk's world and how truly unimportant it has become for ours in comparison. I also learned the importance of watching where you step and minimizing your own noises. I was invited to watch a hunt in a way I had never seen one, which enlightened me. I was educated by a young hawk that was still learning its own way in its world, and because of it I am much more in tune with its world than I had ever been. I continue to learn and grow today because of that experience.

Life and Death

In nature, the difference between life and death can be impacted by so many variables. It can be something that happens in the blink of an eye or something that is a drawn out process. In the end, it is a natural occurrence and beyond the controls and reaches of humans. In the natural world, it is as it must be: for one part to survive another part dies. It isn't any more complicated than that. Or is it?

How are you going to feel and react when you come across these natural events? Will you come upon something that is over and done with that just a carcass remains? Will you hear the sounds of the life and death struggle off in the woods? Will you actually stumble upon the act itself and see the fight for life?

All of these disturbing events can happen and have happened to me over years. Some are truly moving experiences and others left me scratching my head pondering what it must have been like here not too long ago. In the end, it is a chance to see something or hear something that so many never get the chance to be a part of. Therein lays the dilemma you will have when you come face to face with this – the natural struggle for life or death.

Can you handle just being an observer of what is natural or must you interfere and try to be the savior of the species about to be dinner for another? A question you should truly ask yourself before you encounter it.

I think, in my experience, that what you are seeing often makes you react in different ways.   A robin grabbing a worm from the ground likely provokes very little thought from you,

 while a hawk swoopin g in and taking a cardinal probably will conjure up some sadness.

Gulls grabbing a baby duck and bringing it to its death in a

violent manner is something that may make you angry beyond words. A group of coyotes taking down a fawn will give you cause for different thoughts and reactions. The question is what do you do?

I truly struggled with this but in the end I have never interfered. I captured many on film but there were a few I just needed to walk away from as it was a harsh reality I did not wish to watch to completion. For my own inner peace, I needed to turn away.

Here are a few that I have seen that truly were fascinating and held me captive to the bitter end. They all evoked emotions and passion from me. They tugged me in different directions. What would you be feeling, doing?

I was walking along the rocky shore towards rocks where Common Eider, Great Egret, and some gulls were hanging out. I noticed that the eiders had babies and were swimming with them. The parents would dive and the little ones would attempt to, but didn't quite have the hang of it yet. They would wag their little bottoms to try to get under the water but just couldn't make any progress. I smiled and snapped away. The other birds just watched or did their own things. It isn't uncommon to see different species hanging out together. A pair of Black-backed Gulls flew past and began to circle back. Things were about to change in a very big way.

The Black-backed Gull is the largest gull you will see in

(C) 2008 Lloyd W. Alexander

Maine and is also a truly vicious bird. It is not just a scavenger but a predator when the opportunity presents itself. The pair of gulls came back and dove at the adult Common Eiders numerous times, hoping to cause confusion and to separate one baby from the group. The eiders tried to gather up the little ones and herd them towards the rocks. They were using the "safety in numbers" strategy. Soon there was one baby eider separated from the group and the two gulls turned their attention on it. The diving was done as they were now in the water with the baby. The other eiders and birds didn't join in on either side as this assault began. The parents proceeded to herd up the others, apparently knowing the fate of this one lone baby was already decided. The gulls viciously attacked the baby, both tugging it under the water and holding it there as they tried to tear it apart. In the end, they had their meal and it was not an easy thing to watch. I asked myself what I could have or should have done for the baby. While my anger and feeling of helplessness grew, I turned to the other birds. In them I found the answer I was looking for and knew there was nothing that could have been done and that it was as it was supposed to be in the wild. Life and death were just a matter of circumstances of chance and time. The other birds simply watched and the parents seemed simply happy that it was only one that was gone this time.

Another time I saw a Black-backed Gull dive under water and come up with an eel which it eventually swallowed. That was one of the coolest things I have ever seen a gull do. So, why did I have such a different reaction? Is the eel worth less in my eyes than the baby eider? Is it as simple as cute and cuddly versus slimy? Who knows, but the reality of both is exactly the same. The gull needed to eat and it ate what it could to survive, all a natural part of life.

A majestic eagle soars above you and you watch in awe as it moves so effortlessly through the air, twisting and soaring over a lake with its head tilting to spy the water below for its dinner. It begins to descend and you watch in anticipation. Your heart beat picks up as it nears the water. Your eyes widen as it extends its talons and makes contact with the water and you all out jump for joy as it returns to the sky with a fish. "Wow" only begins to scratch the surface of your feelings of exhilaration at such an awesome sight. The timeless icon of America, the beautiful, is right before your very eyes.

Now just change the situation a bit and instead of a fish, the eagle returns to the air with a duckling in those same talons. Do you feel the same exhilaration or has it changed? They are the same to the Eagle. It must eat and an opportunity must be taken.

A fox leaves her den and you watch as the kits come out and play. So very cute and cuddly but also very vulnerable now that mom is out hunting for food. Would you intervene if a fisher or coyote came upon the pups or just sit back and let nature takes its course? The kits may be safe or one may end up as a predator's dinner. You were simply enjoying the beautiful moment when it changed. The fact is, it does change. Does it matter what mom brings back for her kits to eat? Will it change your opinion of the beautiful scene you are being treated to? Nature is nature and things are not as nice and tidy as we would want them to be.

One day while walking I heard a squeak, squeak, squeak that I did not recognize and decided to investigate it. To my amazement I found a National Geographic type image before my eyes, but also a dilemma, as I knew I could easily alter the outcome of this situation. A likely once in a lifetime opportunity or alter nature's course? I chose the only thing I think is true to what I do as a photographer and a naturalist. I watched and took shots of a snake swallowing a frog. The squeak was the frog crying out for help. The snake had a hold of it and

was slowly swallowing it alive. Right before my eyes this situation played out over about five minutes. A truly unique thing to watch unfold and something that normally is missed because we simply do not hear any of the noise or don't look to find it. If I had chosen to save the frog then it lives for another day, but does the snake? I am simply an observer of the struggles between life and death when I am out in the field.

At my home, a goldfinch hit my window on a cold wintery day. I went outside, picked up the bird, and brought it back inside hoping that there was something I could do for it. I cleaned the blood from its mouth and it breathed a tad easier, but I could tell it would not live. I caressed its back and head as I held it in my palm. I whispered to it that it was going to a better place and it would not be alone. The bird took in a deep breath, spread its wings out one last time and as it exhaled its wings closed and the spirit of the bird left too. I held a body now but nothing more. Life and death right in my hands! It was such a powerful and moving experience. I dug a shallow grave in the frozen ground and lined it with leaves and grass before laying the bird in it and covering it with more leaves, grass, and dirt. I knelt down beside the new grave and said a prayer for peace. I could have left the bird to its fate outside in the cold, but in this instance the big difference was that the bird's fate had been decided by hitting a window and that is unnatural to me.

The choice to comfort or ease the pain of an injured or dying animal without altering the course of nature's way is something I am comfortable with doing. To hold the dying bird and give it warmth, love, and tenderness before it passed seemed and felt like the right thing to do. I believe we should care deeply for wildlife and respect what is natural at the same time. We need to be compassionate but also resilient in our letting nature be nature. In that, we shall see true beauty and truly wonderful things that we can barely believe with our own eyes. At other times, we may not understand or may become angry with what we witness, but in the end, we need to let it be just as it was meant to be…wild…to be free to live or die in nature's way.

Cozy As A Fox

There are times in life when you just feel like you have struck gold or won the lottery. This story is one of those times when that was the case, and still today, I have the same feeling. It is a rare thing to come across a person or an animal that you know was just meant to be in your life and that no matter the time apart, the next time you see each other it will be just as wonderful as the last, and that it will seem as though time has not passed at all. A truly blessed feeling you treasure forever.

The first time I met the pair of fox was when I was traveling with my friend Naomi in Crawford Notch, at the start of Crawford Path. The male fox was not shy as he was out in plain sight. I immediately started talking to him and he was extremely curious. It was pretty clear he had learned that hikers have food and that he was clever enough to get some if he just looked cute, which he did very well. I didn't have anything with me but my camera, so I was just talking and taking pictures. The car was not far away though and I did have snacks there. He was busy sniffing the air trying to get a whiff of something delicious that I would share with him. I could tell there was some disappointment that he couldn't smell anything. He turned and walked towards a tree and decided to settle down beside it. I was being given the puppy eyes and was quickly falling in love.

I felt bad and then, out of the corner of my eyes, I saw *her*. I knew that she was something truly special. She was staying just out of direct sight but now that I had spotted her, I could find her and her soft gentle eyes rested upon me. I pointed her out to Naomi but she had seen her too. We both just stood there and enjoyed her playing peek-a-boo with us. I snapped a few pictures of them as they watched us.

For some reason, I believe these two are brother and sister and part of generations of a fox family that is known to live in that area of the mountains. There is plenty of food in the wild for them to capture and eat but there is also a contingent of hikers who travel the trails nearly every day of the year so free food is available as well. It isn't recommended to feed wild animals for many reasons, but that is a point I will not debate one way or the other here. The simple fact is these foxes had obviously been fed for years by hikers and others.

We had been with them for probably a good half hour and it was clear they were comfortable with us and we, of course, were enjoying them. I went back to the car and grabbed some peanuts. I quickly decided to pull out a few shelled peanuts and sit on the ground. As soon as I sat, the male got up and came closer to me, but not so close to not be able to get away quickly. It was great to see they still had a fear of humans. The female came out of the forest, but did not approach us. She was not interested in getting any closer than about thirty yards away and that is where she stayed.

I tossed a few shelled peanuts towards the male and he quickly grabbed them up. I looked at the female and was talking to her, but she did not move to get the food. She was wary of the whole thing and that truly is a good thing. The male kept his distance, but wanted more and was playful in trying to get my attention. A few more were tossed to him and then more time was spent just sitting and observing.

The female seemed to disappear, but then popped up out of the woods from behind the male and snapped at him as she sniffed the ground. I made a motion to toss some peanuts to her, but she bolted as soon as I moved. She was a timid one and that was fine, but it also explained why she was smaller than the male. She was not aggressive in taking steps to get her free handouts. This was a good thing, as she remained wild at heart and kept her distance. Seeing wildlife in the woods is exciting and one of the reasons for people to go into the woods.

In fact, one of the main draws on a few trails is the Gray Jays that meet hikers at known rest areas and try to grab a bite to eat. They will eat from your hand! This behavior is now part of their life and is passed down generation to generation just like I believe has happened with the fox that live near the trails around the Crawford Notch Highland Center. Over the years though, things have changed in the area as humans have built more and more homes. Nature's backyard and the backyards of humans have now become one and the same. So the fox that once were only near trails are now near homes, and the dynamics have changed into one that is a lot less safe for the fox to look for handouts. I will go over that a little later in the story.

I finally got up and went to the area where I had most often seen the female and set some nuts on the large rock there. Then I went back towards the male who had stood up and was watching me. I got his attention and tossed a few peanuts his way so she could get to her stash without him stealing any from her. Slowly she made her way into the open and climbed on top of the rock to grab her peanuts. I smiled as she looked at me the entire time she was eating. As soon as she

consumed the nuts she jumped down and was off, out of sight again.

That was it for giving them food. We just enjoyed watching them as they began to play chase and hide-n-seek it seemed. After they were done with that it was time for naps. The male was fairly close to us and the female was at a very safe distance and in a spot where she could quickly disappear, but for now they both remained in easy view for us.

The sun was setting and the slanting rays settled on the male fox in such a way that it looked as if he was wearing a vest. At that moment, one of my best selling shots was born. The "Vested Fox" has been a best seller and this story of my time spent with him is a favorite of mine to tell.

Soon it was time to leave, as it was getting dark out and the fox can see well at night but Naomi and I were not as fortunate. So, with some sadness, we said goodbye and headed off with a truly wonderful experience to last a lifetime. A sure memory that would always bring a smile to our faces and a picture that would warm others' hearts. It was a great day that would not soon be forgotten.

Winter came and went after what seemed like an eternity. I took a drive, as I often to do, in search of wildlife and anything else beautiful in nature. I was not planning a hike on this day but still went to where the fox had been the previous fall. I hung around but saw nothing and then poked around a little more. Still there was nothing to be found and no immediate signs of recent activity either. I left smiling as I reminisced about our last encounter.

I continued my drive through the notch and stopped at various places, taking pictures of rivers, waterfalls, mountains, and even a moose. It was time to head for the long drive home. I was passing near the fox spot and something inside me said to stop. I pulled over and went up into the area. I saw nothing and waited for about a half hour, enjoying the birds fluttering and singing around me. Then I heard a noise in the trees off to the side. I stared at the bushes and saw a head poke out. It was her; the female fox was still, merely poking her head out of the undergrowth. I felt a wave of emotion engulf me. I felt like I had just found a long lost friend. I said "Hey girl" in an excited voice a few times and to my amazement, she came out from her spot and hurried towards me. She stopped about ten yards away and sniffed the air. She stood there gazing at me and I decided to sit down at the base of a tree. She seemed to be studying me and trying to figure out what to do. I simply continued to talk to her.

In my haste to check out the area I had left my camera behind. While at first I felt a sense of disappointment for not being able to capture the moment, it did not last long. I knew what I was experiencing was truly precious and that it was meant to be just for me. I know that everything is not meant to be captured and shared with the world via photography. Some of these moments are meant to be part of my heart and part of my life forever. The beauty of the moment is to be shared through the joy I have in telling the story.

She came a little closer and sat down. As I spoke, she cocked her head and turned it to and fro as if she was attempting to understand me. It was truly one of the cutest things I had ever seen in my life. I asked where her brother was and how her winter was and basically had myself a one-sided conversation. It may sound funny or odd, but it did not feel like a one-sided conversation. She was listening to me and it felt like she somehow understood that it was a special moment as she lay down and continued to watch me. Slowly she was fading to sleep as cozy as a fox. I just sat there quietly at first, as one of her eyes closed, and then the other. She was sleeping and I was smiling. It felt so wonderful to be trusted and to just enjoy this time with her. No camera and no food to entice her stay either. Only a fox and a man, sitting together in the woods. The feeling of peace and tranquility was a moment to be savored.

Suddenly, her eyes popped open and she stood up. Her head turned towards the trail. I strained to hear what she was hearing, but I simply could not, even when I closed my eyes. She looked back at me as if to say goodbye and then ran into the forest understory, hardly making a sound. Seconds later, I began to hear voices and stood up. A small group of hikers were coming down the trail after a day's hike up to the summits. I walked back to the car feeling like I had just savored a piece of heaven on earth.

I would return to this same spot several more times over the summer and fall, but I never saw her again. I never saw her brother either and wondered what had become of them. I wondered if I would ever see them again or if I would be just left to wonder their fate. I had memories to treasure and ones that would last a lifetime.

Winter came again, and eventually spring, as this is the cycle of nature. My trips would again increase in contrast to the slower winter months. I went to the same spot several times and yelled, "Hey girl", in hopes of seeing her again. She did not come when I beckoned, and each time, my heart filled with more sadness. Where had they gone? Were they ok? On one of my trips, I saw a Ranger's vehicle in a lot near the trail so I pulled in and talked to him for a bit. He said he had heard of a fox recently hit by a car down near the Highland Center, and inside, my body rumbled with emotions. He had not heard anything about any other fox in the area, but he did confirm that this trail was the one that was well known for them being on it, looking for handouts. He agreed it was likely a generational situation and that the comfort with humans was a handed down trait, not a newly acquired one. Fox and other animals cross roads because we put these roads in their habitat and their established paths of travel.

They will always run the risk of being struck by a vehicle. As we claim more and more land, we are leaving them less living space. Our encounters with wildlife are simply unavoidable. The conversation with the Ranger was a pleasant one. If you should ever get the chance to have a chat with one, please do so. They are extremely knowledgeable and do a terrific job.

I had a tough time the rest of the day. Trying to concentrate on looking for other wildlife while appreciating the beautiful scenery, I was caught up in wondering if it was one of the two fox I knew that had been run over. I knew in my heart that it was likely one of them.

I was driving back into Crawford Notch and had that sense about me that I needed to be awake and alert. Then I spotted her on the opposite side of the road, lying in the brown grass. I put on the brakes and backed up. I rolled down the window. She was up and heading towards the woods in a hurry. I yelled, "Hey girl," and she stopped, looking back at me.

I said it again and she turned around and came towards the road. I put up my hands and yelled "Stop"! She seemed to understand and did not move any closer. I pulled the car

around to her side of the road and got out. She was hiding behind a bush and looking up towards the sky as if she were praying. I remember wondering if she was thinking of her brother who must have been the one killed by the car. She had moved down the road quite a ways from where I had seen her the past two times. It was almost like she was moving on from their former spot in a slow year's journey. She looked skinny too. When I got out of the car, I grabbed some hiker's snack and my camera. I snapped a few pictures as she looked at me and then sat down. I softly called to her and she came with her head down and I thought she must be really sad. I talked to her in the gentlest voice I could and she came closer. She looked up and our eyes met. I could see she was sad and yet I knew she was happy to see me. She sat about ten feet away and I did not offer her any food, I simply continued to talk. In fact, she didn't even sniff the air and I have no doubt she would be able to smell the snack I had with me. We just sat there; she, seemingly content to be near me and me content to know I was near her.

After fifteen minutes or so, she moved closer and then even closer. She was near enough that I could reach out and touch her. I talked softly to her and she lay down beside me. I slowly extended my hand and set the food about a foot in front of her. She watched my hand but did not move. I then placed both of my hands on my lap as I sat with crossed legs. She was too close for a picture and it honestly did not seem like it was time for one. This moment wasn't for that anymore. This was a time just to be savored with her being relaxed and close to me. I think perhaps she didn't want to be alone right then. Even though I was a human and could not truly console her, she knew that I was not just another human, but the one that cared about her and the one who could feel what she felt. I understood and I know she knew that. She finally crept close enough to eat.

A SUV pulled over up the road and both of us looked at it for a moment, but it did not move so we went back to enjoying each other. In a couple of minutes, the SUV began to move, and as soon as it did, she looked up at me, as if to say goodbye, and sprinted off into the woods. I watched her go and felt truly sad as she disappeared. She definitely knew this SUV and it was not something she wanted anything to do with. I looked up and saw that it wasn't just another SUV but it was a police officer.

He stepped out and walked to the edge of the road and waved me over. I got up and walked to him. He was not smiling and I was not exactly sure what was coming next. He asked if I was just sitting with a fox, and I of course said yes. There was no doubt he already knew this, but he gets to ask the questions. He asked if I had fed it and I said I had given it some of my snack. He told me that it wasn't a good idea to feed wildlife and that he could give me a ticket for doing so. I told him the story of the fox and I, and he smiled when I was finished. He said he understood, but I still should not feed the fox. He told me he would just give me a warning this time, but not to let him see me doing it again. He said, "I can't tell you not to be close to the fox, but I can tell you not to feed it." I agreed to not give the fox food anymore. He left and I sat back down.

I called to her for a few minutes and then waited for a half hour, but she did not return. He was obviously someone she feared. It was good to know she still feared humans. She was obviously changing her territory each year and I truly felt like this would be the last time I would see her. I was happy and sad about that. A truly awesome thing to be able to be close to the same animal each year, but for her being deeper in the woods, away from all the development, would be the best thing.

I returned this year but have not seen her. I did hear of a fox that is in one of the developments and being fed by some of the people that live there. They feed it cat food and other human foods. In my gut I know it is her and I may try to find her, but in some ways I hope it is not her. I want her to be wild and free, safe from all the possible conflict that awaits her if she stays in the development.

As I said earlier, the notch has changed over the years and is certainly different from when the fox's ancestors first encountered hikers who offered up some of their snacks. The notch was still part of the wilderness then, and the area still wild. Over time, it has become developed and that development has taken away areas that used to belong to nature and its creatures. It is the animals that get blamed for encroaching on the developments or becoming habituated to humans, and yet we are the ones who are in their backyards now and we offer them food. This is why it is not a good idea to feed them, as I have come to learn. We should want them to be as they should be, wild and free. They do not need to depend on us for food, as that only leads to bad things for them, from simply an unhealthy diet, to possible death because someone fears the animal and shoots it. Every situation is different and I am no saint in this myself, but please do not feed them.

I am truly blessed to have been able to share in her life for three straight years in such an intimate way. I will treasure that now and forever. The pictures and the story will be shared  often. Her fate is something that is uncertain at best. If it is her in the development, then I fear a sad ending for my beautiful friend. If she has gone into the wilderness, then her fate shall be as it is supposed to be, as part of a wild animal living in the wilderness and not a wild animal living in a fickle human world where she is precious and novel one moment, and a nuisance and danger the next. Wherever you are my friend, a piece of me forever roams with you.

Wildlife and You

There are few things more exciting than seeing wildlife while out on a hike, a drive, or even in your backyard. It can be a thrilling experience but it also can be an intimidating one. You can greatly increase your chances of viewing wildlife following the tips I am going to share with you. There are things you can do to make the experience a safe one for wildlife and also for yourself.

Seeing beautiful birds and hearing their wonderful song is easiest to do in the spring as they migrate to the Northeast and beyond to have their young. When they arrive, they are at their peak as far as colors go and they are ready to sing away in order to find mates. This generally happens in April and May, give or take a week or so. Check with a local Audubon Society or birding group in your area to get some tips about what to expect in your region at various times of year.

Birds are seldom considered dangerous. Therefore, we may have a tendency to approach them much more closely than they're generally comfortable with. The following are some general guidelines to assist in keeping your viewing experience a positive one for you and one that doesn't disrupt the birds. The first and easiest is to view the birds at a distance with binoculars. This is the most unobtrusive way to watch birds and you will still be able to hear their songs. This allows them to be themselves without fearing you at all.

Another way to observe is to get a little closer by taking a couple of steps, pausing to observe the bird, and make sure it is still comfortable before taking further steps. You still need to maintain a respectful distance even if you think you can keep inching closer. Using binoculars or a camera will help you to maximize your viewing potential without physically infringing on the bird's territory. I have learned that it is extremely important to avoid making eye contact with the bird in order to keep them from flying off. I use a hat with a wide brim to help shield my eyes but still be able to see the bird and this seems to work well. My personal experience has been that, if you make eye contact with the bird, over 90% of them fly off within moments. Binoculars and cameras can have this affect on the birds as well, but it seems to occur less often. It seems that they perceive you as a much greater threat if you make eye contact, and if you think about it, you can probably understand. Humans have hunted and captured birds for a long time and thus, if they see you looking at them, then they may think you have an ulterior motive. Their natural instincts have developed over time to ensure their greatest chance of survival.

Keep your camera and binoculars close at hand so the movement to reach for it is not a long one, as the shorter the movement, the better. Also make sure your movements are slow. Anything fast and they are off for sure. If it is nesting season or they have babies in the nest, you should keep your distance as you do not want disturb them during this important time. This could also lead a predator to the nest with the scented trail you leave behind. Other scenarios could include some parents leaving the nest and not coming back or you could cause a newborn to accidentally fall out of the nest. So be cautious during the summer months if you come across a nest. Should a bird dive at you, move away from the area as you are too close for its comfort. Always respect the birds' space. Wait until the fall to check out a nest, as it will be empty, but please leave the nest as you found it in case that particular bird species reuses its nest the following year.

It is important when you enter an area to let things calm down and get back to what is normal for the birds. Birds will know you are there and will likely remain hidden for a few minutes. If you are still, they will slowly come back out and go about their business. You can get birds to be more visible by calling to them. There are many ways to do this and some are more controversial than the others.

The first is called pishing, which is a noise that arouses curiosity in birds. Many times they come into the area to check out the unfamiliar noise. It has been explained to me several different ways. I am not sure if it is known if pishing truly resembles anything specific, other than unfamiliar noises, but there are various theories which you may research and decide for yourself. The following is a section on how to pish which is quoted from birding.about.com

How to Pish

Pishing is an easy technique to master and many birders have their own sounds that work best in the field. Different sounds can be effective, though most are made with the teeth together and repeated 3-5 times in a slow, regular tempo. Changing the tempo or adding additional sounds to each pish sequence can also entice birds to respond.

The most common pish syllables include:

Pish

Pssst

Sip

Seep

Kissing noises, tongue clicks and a rapid "chit-chit-chit" noise are pishing alternatives that can also get the attention of curious birds.

The volume of the pish should be kept at or slightly softer than a conversational tone. Birds have excellent hearing and very loud pishes are likely to chase birds away rather than attract them. Similarly, too much pishing can easily desensitize the birds to the noise and they will no longer respond.

I feel pishing is very effective to get some activity going on around you. Once the activity begins, stop pishing and see what happens, as usually the birds make their own sounds and more birds will come around. Sometimes you can draw them in a bit closer with a few extra pishes, just don't overdo it. Remember that there is no set noise, so try various sounds to see what results you may get.

You can also take pishing to the next level and mimic a bird's call. This can be hard to do but it is something you can learn with practice. This is something that I believe should only be done in the spring and fall. If the birds are in nesting season, which is generally thought of as summer, then it is best to leave them be and not make them think another bird is near as they may leave the nest to chase it away. This leaves the nest vulnerable plus wastes precious energy the bird needs for the job of keeping eggs warm or finding food for the young. Often birds are quieter in the summer as they no longer need to advertise to find a mate and do not want potential predators alerted to their nest location.

Electronic devices that have recorded bird songs and calls on them can also be used to call birds closer. This is a more controversial subject but often gets a species to respond. Again, best not to do this in the summer. Any sound you play should be played low and only a few times. If the bird is there it will hear the sounds, and if it wants to come check it out, you can be assured it will do just that. Again, there are many thoughts and theories on what playing the call actually does to the bird, so you must be watching for obvious signs of stress. These can be as simple as the bird puffing itself up when it's near you, flying back and forth quickly, or incessant calling of its own. If in any way you feel that you are stressing the bird, stop. Do not continue to play the recording or pish. It is extremely important to remember that in the spring, many birds are arriving from wintering grounds. They are establishing territories and looking for mates for summer reproduction. In the fall, birds are getting ready to migrate back to their wintering grounds and need to build their energy reserves for this trip. So please realize that you could be making the birds' waste valuable energy needed during all seasons of the year.

One other thing to consider is what call or mimic you are using. It is certainly fun to see hawks, various raptors and owls but remember, they eat other birds, so be careful where and when you do this as you may inadvertently cause the demise of one bird to feed another. Always think of possible consequences before you make any mimic calls.

If you are with a group, then pishing is generally accepted as ok. However, you should ask before mimicking, and definitely ask before using a recording. Some take offense to it and since it is for all of us to enjoy you should consider the feelings of others.

Finding wildlife and having a safe encounter with them is extremely rewarding but is also more challenging and takes more practice than with birds. You must be alert and ready for whatever may happen, so thinking ahead and considering the possible outcomes is a must. Remember, you are in their backyards so to speak and respect must be given to them. You are the intruder and the outsider in their eyes.

I cannot stress the importance that you are not to make direct eye contact with wildlife as it can be perceived as a threat to them, and more times than not, their experiences with humans have likely not been good ones. So they may already be on edge and meeting eyes can trigger a fight or flight reaction. That being said, you must also keep your eyes on the animal and watch for signs of what it might be thinking. Over time, with much experience and practice, you may be able to make eye contact. Take some time first to learn how to observe an animal in a non-threatening way and be able to evaluate each situation. No two situations are alike.

How does the animal appear to you when it sees you? Surprised? Scared? Indifferent? Most animals are going to keep a cautious eye on you and try to read you as you try to read them. During this evaluation period you need to have a clear, calm mind. If you are projecting your fear or any negative thoughts, the animal will pick up on it and will react accordingly; do not underestimate what wildlife can perceive. So calm yourself and slow your heartbeat with deep, relaxing, quiet breaths. You want the animal to feel you are stress-free and calm in its presence and that you mean it no harm.

Also look at the body posture of the animal to help judge what it is feeling. Has it tightened itself up, compacted like it could surge? Is its body weight distributed evenly or on one leg or a set of legs? Is there hair that is raised or standing? Is it making any noises?

If it is compacted, it could be afraid of you and assessing the situation. Slowly move backwards to give it more space and see if the body posture changes. No sudden movements! Go slowly and methodically, with your eyes remaining on the animal but not its eyes. After you back up, it is possible the animal may run or it may settle. Depending on the reaction, you may need to back up further. Be mindful of where you back up and make sure there is room behind you to keep moving and that you do not back yourself in a corner. Always assess your surroundings.

Check the body weight and see if it is evenly spread or shifted to a certain part of the body. If it is evenly distributed, then it is unlikely anything is going to happen at that moment. For example, if you are standing with your legs shoulder width apart, it is hard for you to make a quick movement. Other things happen first such as shifting your weight, and the same is true for animals. So if the animal has its weight on its front legs, it may be thinking, prepared to run away at a moment's notice, as it is easy to push off those front legs away from you with a quick muscle movement. If the weight is shifted to the hind legs, then be very careful as the direction of movement is likely going to be forward. It may be forward and then turn, but you do not know if it will turn and should be prepared that you are in its potential path. Each animal requires a different reaction if it charges you and you should read up on this from an expert on the subject or ask your local Ranger what you should do if you encounter such and such. I am not going to offer you advice on what to do if something charges as I am not an expert. I have only been charged once and it was by a rabid beaver.

If the hair on the animal is raised or it is making noises, these are signs it is uncomfortable and you should move back to give it more space. The animal does not want to attack you but does want more distance between you and it, so listen to what it's telling you and back up. When something is frightened, the more room you give it the better. Be sure that you back away slowly, facing the animal and not exposing your back, as this is often seen as a sign of weakness.

You should also try to have a general idea as to when animals will likely have their young with them, and know that during that time, they will be much more on edge. Many are also on edge during mating season. Bull Moose in particular can be very aggressive during their mating season which is in the fall. If you see the young, but not the parent, please back away and listen for mom as she is near and you do not want to be between her and her young. Doing so may provoke an aggressive response. Many animals grunt at you when they are warning you and some stomp their feet, but there is no steadfast rule they will do this before their fight or flight impulse kicks in. Use caution and respect the distance.

There is no exact way, while in the wilderness, to know if an animal is rabid but when observing an animal take into consideration the following. How does its fur look? Mangy is not good but you also need to keep in mind many animals shed their coats in spring and fall. So fur can look unkempt but not really dirty or mangy. If it is mangy, i.e. excessively dirty and/or shabby in appearance, be very careful. Is the animal drooling or does it have foam around its mouth or nose? This is a sign of an unhealthy animal, but remember that this sign is not always present in a rabid animal. An animal with rabies may also come towards you and display no fear or hesitancy which is not normal of most animals. If you encounter an animal that looks sick or you suspect may be rabid avoid it and move away from it. Report it to the authorities.

It is important to consider where you are and where the animal is as well. What you are concentrating on is: what is the best route for the animal to take to remove itself from the situation. The animal will look for the easiest regress. If you are blocking the easiest egress, the animal must decide whether to go through where you are or take a more difficult, and possibly unsafe, route away from you. You could accidentally be making the animal feel cornered despite the fact that you are in the middle of nowhere. You are probably wondering how.

Let's say we come across a bear that is eating blueberries on the edge of a field. On one side is a fairly steep hill, on the other side is thick forest, behind the bear is a slope that goes down to a river, and then there is you with a meadow behind you. Where is the bear most likely to wish to go? Steep hills and thick forest are certainly possible and provide cover, but getting through both requires quite a bit of work. The river requires even more work and this is why where you stand is the best escape route. So if the bear decides it needs to run, it is quite possible it is going to run right at you to avoid being slowed by the other obstacles. It likely wants nothing to do with you but could bump you as it goes past. If you get hurt then the bear is likely to be called a danger to humans and will be moved to a different area or put down by Rangers. The bear may also choose one of the other routes because it's more afraid of a confrontation with you than the potential dangers it could encounter. That may cause it to injure itself by going in the less desirable direction. So there are two things you can do to make this better for both of you. Move to either side of the meadow, so the bear has plenty of space to leave the situation safely. You also must leave yourself room for a safe exit as well. The other option is to simply leave and be thankful you had the chance to view the bear. We are not always afforded the opportunity to watch any animal for extended periods of time. Remember, take what is given.

It is great to come across wildlife on the side of the road as it often means you get great views because the roadside is clear of trees and you are close without having to approach the animal. When you encounter an animal beside the road, there are things to consider in order to keep the animal safe. The safety of any other vehicles that arrive while the animal is there must also be considered. First, remember your car should be pulled off to the side of the road. Stopping in the middle of the road or only partly off the road is a danger to both yourself and oncoming traffic. You also may put on your hazard lights, warning oncoming drivers to be alert. If you choose to get out of your vehicle, keep yourself or your car between the animal and the road. You may also use your car as a safety for yourself and stay near it, but make sure you are not in the road either. If you choose to approach the animal, remember to watch the animal's signs just as you would if you found it while on a trail. It is important to make sure that your presence in no way causes the animal to run towards the road. That is a potentially deadly scenario for both the animal and oncoming traffic. Enjoy the view but don't overstay to the point of causing the animal to run off, especially if the road is the easiest route of regress for the animal.

Feeding wildlife is also something you should not do as it can eventually cause problems. It is likely to encounter numerous humans as more and more people hike trails and climb mountains. The wilderness is a bit less wild as a result of us being there all the time. We do not want to have wildlife associate humans with a quick easy meal so handouts should not be given. An animal that gets used to humans and associates them with food is bound to get in trouble as not all humans will tolerate them. A bear that has become habituated to humans and associates them with a free handout may enter campgrounds to get the food and not be scared off when people try to make it go away. They may also smell food in your backpack and follow you on the trail waiting for you to give it food. Think about how scary that would be as you would not know the bear's intention. The same thing applies with any other animal. Seeing them is great, but being followed by them is unnerving and likely will result with the animal being labeled as a "problem animal" which will need to be dealt with by Rangers. Currently, in the White Mountains, there are a few trails that have signs warning that bears may follow you for food because they have been fed and are now associating hikers' backpacks as easy food sources.

Many times when you encounter wildlife, you will likely get the urge to try and get closer. I do not recommend this as they are wild and their behavior is simply unpredictable. It is best to keep a safe distance and let the animal decide if it wants to move a little closer. Watch for the signs, and if it is appearing relaxed and going about its business, then enjoy the encounter. Just remember that it is wild and things can change in the blink of an eye, so keep a distance that is safe and smart.

So when you encounter wildlife, remember, it is a gift and not something that you should take for granted as an everyday event. Appreciate and respect the animal while you are with it and watch for signs to make sure you and the animal remain safe. Check out the area and make sure you are allowing the animal safe passage to leave if it feels the need to do so. Be aware, be alert, be smart, and enjoy.

Fawntastic

I had been on a mission to see and photograph a fawn. I had never seen one in the wild before so it would be quite the big deal for me. It was the right time of the year for it and I was seriously searching. Something I normally do not do is look for one specific animal, as it always seems to block my vision to other gems that might be in plain sight. I was beginning to think it wouldn't happen so I went to the Maine State Wildlife Park in Gray, as they always seem to have fawns each year. I was amazed to find out that the wildlife park did not have a single one and I was beginning to understand that I was simply too focused on one thing and missing so much else. I began to think things were just not going to go my way and I would have to wait for things to happen on their own time, so I refocused on being open to everything around me.

Then, on a trip to NH, I saw a fawn off to the side of a dirt road and quickly pulled the car over to the roadside. I slowly moved into position to get a shot, but off it darted into the woods. There wasn't a lot of sound and I was sure it had not gone far, so I moved a little closer, but then something inside of me said not to follow it and that this was not the one for me to photograph; this was just one for me to see and enjoy with my own eyes for those brief moments. I often get these intuitions and I do listen to them all of the time. It could have been that by following, I would have spooked it further and sent it somewhere it shouldn't go. Perhaps then a predator would be onto it or some other life altering event could occur. These are things I would never know, but I trust when I am getting the feelings to do, or not do, something. So I simply stopped and went back to the car.

Nearly a week later, I was coming out of the woods near home and saw another fawn with its mom. I got into position to take some photos and they disappeared into the woods near some houses. I again decided it just wasn't a good spot to go looking, since Route 25's fast moving commuter traffic was not far away. The safety of the animals and others must always come into your mind when in these situations. It is great to get an awesome image, but not at the expense of causing a tragic event. Another thing to consider when looking for that great view or great shot is whose property you're on. Even if it is not marked "no trespassing", you should ask before going onto someone else's property. This will take a few extra moments, but if it is meant for you to see, then the animal will still be there and you won't be making it harder for the next photographer or casual observer.

The deer were gone from sight, but I was thankful for the little view I had of them. I was now getting glimpses, when I had been coming up empty, and I certainly was thankful for what I was getting and that was part of the lesson for me. It was a reminder that simply being able to see this beauty in a natural setting was a gift all in itself that should be appreciated and not overlooked.

I later was fortunate to receive a call from the Maine State Wildlife Park in Gray. They had just received a fawn into the facility. Often a person will come across a fawn that is alone and call the Game Warden or try to help it by taking it to their home or to a Warden Station, and the fawns will often end up at facilities such as the wildlife park. The intent is great and well meant, but more times than not, this is a big mistake, as what the fawn really needs is to be left where it is. It is very likely what mom has done is left the fawn in a safe place, as does (females) will "stash" their young while they forage for food and return to feed them. If you should stumble upon a fawn alone, this is the most likely scenario and you should leave it alone or call a wildlife official to let them make a determination. After you have touched or moved the fawn, it is often in much greater danger from predators that will follow the scented trail you left behind. So please think twice before moving any young animal you find. Since there was one at the wildlife park now, I planned on heading there within the next few days to get the shots of my fawn.

It was the time of the year for deer to have had their babies as was evident by the glimpses I was seeing, but my faith in photographing one in the wild was fading and I had begun to resign myself to the notion that perhaps my only photos of a fawn would come from the wildlife park. Mother Nature had other ideas in mind, and my luck was about to change in a very big way, but it would not be without lessons learned. These were lessons I should have already mastered, but in my excitement at spotting a fawn, those lessons learned had become lessons lost. It would become clear that these lessons were not missed by Mother Nature.

I was in North Conway, having a delicious pizza with a friend, when I received a text message. I hesitated and thought about not looking at it, but it just seemed to be begging me to read it. I picked up the phone and read the text. Naomi quickly said, "A fawn, huh"? I shook my head yes emphatically. She knew how diligently I had been hunting for one. She had been asking everyone near her home in Berlin if they had seen any fawns, trying to aide in my search. The text was from a person who lived near where I did in Steep Falls. She frequently saw deer near her home which bordered woods and is a perfect habitat. I replied to the text and said thank you, but I didn't say I would be able to make it.

It was late in the afternoon, but it was summer, so the sun wasn't going to set for quite some time. Despite the urge to head off on the journey, I decided it would likely be in vain as I was over an hour away. I reasoned a fawn would not be allowed to stay in the open that long. So I set the phone down and took a long draw off of my refreshing soda.

Naomi looked at me and smiled. She said, "Well, what are you waiting for?" and I wondered for a second myself. Then I said, "It wasn't the same as the bear in Pinkham Notch and I just didn't feel it would be there when I got there." She gave me a look I had seen before and it was the look of "Is that REALLY what you are thinking"? It actually was, and as I picked up a fresh slice of pizza, I think she believed me. So we ate and enjoyed the meal. The pull in the back of my mind was there, as excitement and possibility tried to overtake the reasoning I was using that the fawn would not be there. The pizza was really good though and I did eat it kind of fast. After the pizza, we went outside and tried to decide what else to do, but it quickly became clear to both of us that I was heading home in search of the fawn. I have to say I am thankful for such an understanding friend who encouraged me to go for it. I was ready to pass up the chance, but she wouldn't let me. Thanks!

Off I went to Route 113 in North Conway, headed for Fryeburg. As I neared the Maine/New Hampshire border, I spotted a beautiful American Kestrel, a small falcon, sitting on a tree just beside the road. It was looking for prey and the light was amazing. It would be a beautiful photograph. I started to slow down to take what was given me, but my mind said Go! Go! Go! I pushed the pedal down and accelerated off down the road. The kestrel kept popping into my mind as I went further and further away from it. I didn't take what was given and I wondered if that was going to be ok, as I know it has not been before. Did I pass up a beautiful kestrel to miss a fawn? Would that be my lesson?

I drove on and after a brief stop home I was finally near my destination, turning onto one of the last roads before I would arrive. There it was, right there on the side of the road in a small clearing. All alone and grazing on lush green grass was a fawn with its beautiful white polka dotted coat. My jaw must have dropped to the floor as I pulled the car to a stop and turned it off. I reached for the camera and took a couple shots before slowly, quietly, getting out of the car. The fawn looked up at me and I thought it would run. I quietly said, "It is ok. I won't hurt you. Please stay for a minute." The fawn's ears

twitched as it heard my voice and its posture relaxed a bit as well. It would stay and I would get my images too. I snapped and snapped. Then I just stood and admired as it slowly began to walk towards the woods with legs that seemed too thin to be able to hold it up.

Another car approached and began honking its horn which scared the fawn, and it bolted away to the woods. I really never understand these people, as I am not hunting and I would never hurt an animal. Maybe for them it is a joy to ruin a moment. I guess that is an answer to a question that I will never know.

One thing you should think about when you come upon someone who appears to be watching something off the side of the road is that you should respect the fact that they are watching the animal and do as little as possible so as not to disturb the situation. Instead of backing up, just simply pull over slowly, turn off the car, remove your keys from the ignition, gently open and close the door, and walk back on the opposite side of the road of the animal as quietly as you possibly can. More times than not, the chances of you both seeing the treasure decrease greatly if you stop your car quickly, open and shut the doors loudly or walk with scuffling feet as this is likely to alarm the animal. If this is going to be your approach, then you might as well just keep driving because the animal will bolt.

I got back in the car and continued heading to my friend's home. Another text came in and all it said was "twins." My face lit up as I turned down her drive and looked to see if I could find anything in the woods

There were some deer there, but no fawns that I could see. I parked and Dawna came out all smiles, showing me a couple pictures she had taken and then letting me know where they had gone.

I thanked her and slowly moved in the direction of a small hill. On top of the hill I could see the fawns clearly and they were heading towards me with their mom. I backed away to let them have their trail and watched as they came by me. I snapped some photos and was getting some looks from mom, but it all worked out as I kept my distance and did not make eye contact with her.

There are times you truly need to read the animal and have a feel for the situation. I had been here many times and mom knew who I was, and while eye to eye contact would normally be fine, I knew this wasn't our normal situation. The two little ones added to the equation changed the game, and her place was not simply a deer in a herd, but a mom with two little ones to worry about. So it was best for me to play shy, showing her she was boss. Eye contact can quickly be interpreted as a sign of aggression or a challenge in different situations, and this was one of them. Learning to read an animal's signals is important, and I have taken a lot of time to read and to study when I am with animals or birds. I let them tell me how close or how far we need to be and how long I can stay. I feel I am lucky to be in their world and it is up to me to understand it.

I turn and there is a third fawn now, and I take a few more shots. I am ecstatic as I saw four fawns after having seen none, and even had a great dinner with a friend! Just as I think I have everything to be smiling about, the kestrel appears in my mind. I didn't take what was given, but I was still given all this amazing stuff. How could that be and what would the price end up being?

I thanked Dawna and went home to process the images. I was up late, as the excitement of the day's occurrences was there with every image I looked at. I felt like I was on cloud nine. The next day I woke early and headed to the ME/NH border on Route 113 with Michelle, as it was a Saturday and she was off work; plus it was a good day to take Molly, our dog, for a ride. As I reached the area, the kestrel was still there, so I drove past it and turned around. I got out of the car and did my usual approach, but with just mere steps into the field the bird flew off yet remained in sight. In fact, it had only flown out of camera distance. I went back to the car and had Michelle take Molly to the little beach down the road. I would walk the half mile or so from the NH border to the beach in Maine.

The kestrel stayed still except for its head which was clearly turned to watch me as I approached. I was able to get closer this time, and as I raised the camera, it flew off again but stayed within sight. I smiled and was pretty sure I understood that I was being taught a lesson.

I continued walking and again I was allowed to get closer to the bird, but as soon as the lens came up, the bird flew off with a shriek. The shriek might have been a laugh if a kestrel could actually laugh. This was clearly the kestrel acting out of the ordinary, but with a purpose that I was clearly beginning to understand.

I walked again, and this time the kestrel was on the other side of the road. I could tell that either way this would be the last chance for a picture, as behind it was the forest, and once it went there, our time together would be done. As I crossed the road I looked directly at the kestrel and said I was sorry and I should not have taken it for granted the day before. I understood that I had not taken what was given. The kestrel turned its head side to side as if listening to me, and then gave another shriek as it leapt off the branch and flew over my head. I turned and watched as it turned and headed back towards me, flying lower and lower till about head height. I wasn't quite sure what was going to happen, but I knew my knees were feeling a tad bit wobbly as I could see the talons. It lifted past me and landed in the tree.

I paused for a couple of seconds in amazement at what had just happened. I walked slowly, looking up at the kestrel. I raised the camera and the raptor stayed still. I snapped one shot and then it lifted off and glided into the woods. I was able

111

to get a taste of the beauty I had passed over in my haste and understood the point. I truly needed to remember to take what was given, when it was given, and not just hope it would be given again another day.

The kestrel was truly stunning and I was fortunate that it was still there the following day, and I felt privileged that it allowed me to get even one shot. Mother Nature had shown me the error of my ways and led me down a path of humility and appreciation. FAWNTASTIC!

Fools Rush In

Have you ever done something and then looked back and wondered: "What you were thinking"? Surging forward, fueled by adrenaline, only to later experience all of the fear you left behind come flooding back? Sometimes you just seem to lose sight of the sanity of a situation and venture beyond your normal comfort zone. This seems to be something that happens to me quite often. I, of course, do not recommend doing any of this the way I have done it. Heck, I still can't believe I did it! In truth, I am lucky to have come out of these situations without being seriously injured or even killed.

I always talk about being prepared and knowing when it is time to simply turn around. The trail will always be there another day and the key is to make sure you are still alive and healthy when the day is done so you can return another day. Early on in my hiking career, I really thought I could push through anything and that there were no limits. If I could just get my mind over any fear, the danger would never be as bad as I imagined it could be. How unrealistic was that!

I look back now and think about what an idiot I was and how far off that kind of thinking was from reality. I was hiking in the winter and it had been an average winter, but in the mountains, average isn't the same as average near sea level. Rain at sea level rarely means rain on a mountain, as it is colder at higher altitudes. While it may be raining along the coast, it is more likely to be snowing in the mountains, especially the higher up you get. Somehow, I did not quite get that, and my winter hiking experience was basically "hills" and small mountains and not the larger mountains where the conditions are vastly different. Smaller hills and mountains still offer some cover in the way of trees, while on the larger mountains you are more exposed to the elements as you pass into the alpine zone.

I set out on my first adventure with South Moat Mountain near North Conway as my destination. It promised great views with 2770 feet of elevation gain and a six mile round trip. It sounded very much in my comfort zone for a hike. The top also boasted of 360 degree views because it was an exposed rock top. This mountain was an example of what I considered to be a "hill" as it does not pass through an alpine zone. To prepare for the hike, I read recent trail reports which said it was mostly bare bootable and straightforward to the top. To me, this meant that a lot of extra equipment such as crampons, ice ax, and snowshoes were not needed. The weather called for rain the next day so I figured I would go after the storm passed.

It was about forty five degrees Fahrenheit when I left the house early in the morning. It looked to be a superb day. I had packed everything the night before and had plenty of food and water. A few extra layers of clothing were in my pack as well. I was eager and the drive was a relaxed one until I neared the mountain and then my adrenaline started to kick in. Your mentality changes and a transformation takes place as you change the music to something inspiring and you begin to believe you can conquer mountains. Radio blasting with the bass pounding, I pulled to a stop near the trailhead.

I finished Metallica's 'Enter Sandman' and burst from the car with energy and confidence. I made sure I had everything and noticed my stabilizers (soles with upside down screws on the bottom that attach to your boots) were not packed, but remembered the trail report and decided that I probably would not need them. Let me point out here that this is a huge miscalculation and one I hope none of you make. Please do not underestimate what conditions you may find on the trail. A trail report is a good piece of information that will give you a general view of conditions you might face, however, the weather in the mountains is always changing and thus the reports grow old quickly. The fact is, you need to prepare for the worst and nothing less. On that day, I should have brought my stabilizers and snow shoes and crampons too. Hiking requires you to be smart and it is always better to be safe than sorry. My mistakes made it so I came very close to being beyond sorry.

Some of you who are not experienced hikers may be wondering why you would need so many pieces of equipment for your feet alone. Each serves a very different purpose and using them at the right time will make you safe. Crampons are basically steel teeth that you attach to the sole of your boot which are very useful when there is a hard ice surface. Stabilizers are basically upside down screws on a sole that you strap to your boots which helps you get traction on slippery surfaces, but do not dig in as deep as crampons when on icy and elevated terrain. Snowshoes are designed to prevent you from sinking deep in the snow on surfaces that are soft or crusty. In general, they will not work well on icy surfaces. Please understand, this is a very brief overview of these pieces of equipment and you should read further or ask a guide to get a better understanding of their full use.

I hit the trail with just my boots and figured it would be great. It didn't appear that it had snowed on the mountain but had rained a little and actually packed things down. This was a sign that I missed back then. Rain at a low elevation could mean ice or snow higher up the mountain and better coverage for my feet should have been a no brainer. I made good time on the packed trail and decided to take a rest before hiking up a section that looked a tad steep. I found a tree to sit on but found I could not sit on it as the tree was covered in about a third of an inch of ice. The ground had become kind of crunchy as well with a thin layer of crust. These were signs I simply ignored either out of stupidity or simply a lack of understanding what conditions around me actually meant. Winter hiking is completely different than any other time of year. Now that I understand it better, it is my favorite time of year to hike. However, you must understand and educate yourself about the differences by either taking courses or reading books on the subject.

117

After a snack and water, I headed up the steep section as it twisted and turned, and I could feel my legs getting a workout and my lungs pleading for more air. The cold seemed to sting deep in my lungs as the temperature at higher elevations is much colder which is to be expected. The higher I went the colder it was getting but I was prepared for that. I stopped and added a layer of clothing. The crust on the ground was getting thicker, slowly turning to ice and I began to wonder if I should have brought my stabilizers, but it was too far to go back and get them. I would have to call it a day. Here is the first time insanity or bravado took over for reality. Truth is, I should have turned around, but I told myself it must change to snow above and I could handle it. The winds had picked up and the top was probably bare rock since the snow had likely been blown off by the strong winds…so it would be a walk in the park. I had just irrationally rationalized going on. I continued upward.

I trekked up the slopes and soon found myself having to take smaller steps to keep my weight well balanced on a crust that was getting harder to break through. I could see out beyond the trees now. The view was nice and I desired to see more of it. I began to kick step my way upward as the terrain was gaining altitude at a steep angle. Kick stepping is making a foot hold with your boot by kicking through the ice or snow rather than just trying to maneuver over the ice or unstable surface. The summit appeared to be right ahead, but I needed a break again as working my way upward had been tiring. Each step had to be planned and then made, rather than just walking on up.

The voices called to me from each shoulder.... the sensible hiker and the thrill seeking hiker....with bits of information as to what I should be doing. In my stomach, I felt turmoil, in my heart, a fast heartbeat, and in my mind, confusion. Sensibility seemed to be competing with a side that was insensible. "I can do it" and then "I can't do it". "Sure you can, as you can do anything". The other side begged that I look at the conditions and the increasing ice which made each step a gamble. Bravado asked, "What will I say to those who knew I was hiking today if I go back down and do not summit". Will they think I am weak, or worse, think I am afraid"? I was putting peer pressure on myself now! Bravado won.

I stood up and decided to plow onward. I made progress, but over time it slowed considerably as the conditions worsened. I was out of the woods, enjoying the scenery, so I pressed on. I could see the summit and finally crested the last bit, thinking I had reached my goal. I got there, but stopped in my tracks. It was a false summit and again my mind began to race, as before me was a skating rink for which I was not prepared! The rocks certainly were not bare, as I had theorized they would be, but were covered in a sheath of ice. I was not sure if it was something I could break through. False courage prevailed, speaking loud and clear. While I should have been afraid, I was not. My mind had turned this into a battle of me versus the mountain, and the summit would be mine! Looking back, it was so easy to let me sucker myself into this position. I can't believe I was so ready to push aside safety for fear of what others might say if I didn't succeed or let the adrenaline of being near the top push aside the last bit of reason that I had. I was not brave, but I sure was stupid, and losing IQ points with each step.

I moved on, as the real summit had to lie just ahead and I couldn't turn back now. At first, I could break through the ice to a layer of snow and I was still able to move comfortably. Actually, more comfortably than the steep face of the climb I had done just moments ago. My mind began to ease, but I should have been paying attention to the wind picking up and the clouds moving in. The snow below the ice quickly faded away with each step until just ice remained. I paused for a breath and studied the clouds that were closing in around me. I knew I could make it to the summit and get back to the trees before any storm could make it to me. Again, looking back, another big mistake! I am not a weatherman and while the weather did not call for any precipitation that day, the mountains often have weather that changes quickly and does not match the forecast of the land below. I should have turned around, but I did not.

I was at the base of a little incline and was sure I would see the summit on the other side. The problem now was two layers of ice were below my feet and the top layer was brittle. The trick was for me to step on the ice with enough pressure to move forward and to overcome the fear of stepping on the ice and slipping as the top layer broke away. So now what....turn around.....hell no....I was just about there and there was no way I was turning around! Looking down either side, it would have been a long and painful slide. It likely would not have killed me, but it could have hurt me severely and left me stranded for sure. Sensibility was out and adrenaline was in as I began to

121

crawl slowly up the incline digging my hands and sides of my feet into the icy mountain. I finally reached the top of the incline and could see the summit and the drop off on the other side before the rest of the mountain range continued. So all I had left to hike was a slight decline then another incline with some fairly flat space in between. Ok, doable, right? Right, is what I told myself. My stomach tossed and turned and was probably objecting, but adrenaline kept pumping. I slid down the decline on my butt and it was kind of fun, but again not very smart, as I did not have a way to stop myself should I have veered off track.

I stood and tried to walk, but quickly found I could not keep my balance and decided crawling would work. I crawled and crawled till I got to the summit. The clouds were becoming thick and the winds were gusting strong. I stood on the summit and enjoyed what was left of the view. A gust of wind sent my feet scrambling for something solid but they only found ice and I fell onto my knees. Dumb luck is all that kept me from sliding off the summit. That was when I realized I was not in control of the situation and that I was walking the fine line between risk and reward. Suddenly, the situation had crossed over to all risk. Snow began to spit from the sky and I knew that spelled even more trouble for me. Sense came back to me, slapping me with a wave of fear that made my whole body tremble. I looked down to where I had come from and where I now had to return to, and all I could see was danger. My friend bravado was nowhere to be found, and trust me, I was looking for him because I wanted to kick his butt! Over time, I have learned fear can do a few things to you. It can freeze you in your tracks and lock down your mind so you simply can't do anything. Or it can work to your benefit to keep you from getting into trouble should you choose to listen to it. Well for me, I was past the point of trouble and while I most definitely wanted to stay right where I was, I also knew that was not an option, especially with snow beginning to fall. I needed to get going as the snow would make the ice even dicier.

I decided the best way to get back down from the summit was to just slide down on my hands and knees backwards and then crawl up the next incline, and repeat this process till I was off the slippery summit. I did this as controlled as possible till I was able to get back off of the rocky top of the mountain. Once I was back down to tree line, I knew I was going to be fine and just let my body collapse into the snow. I was exhausted mentally and physically. My knees were quite sore and my back, neck and shoulders were stiff from trying to hold them rigid for so long. I closed my eyes as the snow fell on my face. I made a promise to myself that I would always be more prepared from that point onward and that I would allow myself to turn around before reaching a summit if necessary. Live with the dignity of self-preservation rather than die as a fool.

I wish I could say that was the only foolish thing I have done in my time outdoors, but it is not and we all have lessons to learn. When it comes to the outdoors, it is advantageous if you learn these lessons prior to heading out into the wild and form a plan that is well prepared and logical.

I was traveling down Route 113 one afternoon during hunting season, when I saw a Bull Moose just off the road. I do not hunt, but do love to interact with nature and love to take pictures of the encounters. It came towards the road and I snapped a few pictures…no big deal. But then, it crossed the road about thirty feet in front of me and the adrenaline began to pump. The huge animal began to trot and disappeared between two trees. Suddenly I found myself jogging after the moose with my camera in hand. Again, that sensibility thing seemed to vanish.

I could hear plenty of crashing, banging, and snapping as we went. I was right behind it and yet I could not see it. I remember thinking, "How could something so big be right in front of me, but yet not be in my view?" So I picked up the pace as I searched before me, all senses on alert. Once again rational thought seemed to have escaped me and was replaced by the urge to capture the image of this giant of the forest on film. A vision of the magnificent photo I was seeking was all I could imagine as I ran blindly forward.

Suddenly, it was quiet and I realized I was the only one making noise. I broke through the brush into an opening and stopped short. I was suddenly face to face with the moose and his big ole rack!   My knees became very weak. Our eyes met and I could see that he was not really pleased that I was running after him. I could also sense that it was aware that I did not intend it harm. However, it still had a lesson to teach me about respecting an animal's space, as it stomped its hoof and snorted at me loudly.

I was shaking but managed to talk quietly to the moose, in hopes of what I wasn't sure, but it is all that came to mind. I said I was sorry, and boy, did I mean it! I profusely thanked him for not charging me which brought another less forceful snort. I think we had reached an understanding that I was an idiot and it was about time for me to be on my way. I slowly backed up and continued to say I was sorry. As soon as I felt the brush touch the back of my legs I turned sideways. I bowed to the moose and said goodbye. I felt safe then as I knew if it had wanted to harm me it would have already done so. It just wanted me gone. I turned my back to it and listened as I walked away. I could hear it going through the brush and woods away from me.

I made it back to my car and felt like slapping myself upside the head as I knew I had just been a total idiot again. I chased a Bull Moose into the woods during hunting season with no orange on and this made me a target to hunters too. On top of that, it was rutting season and the bulls are not predictable at all and, in fact, it is when they are most dangerous. Their testosterone is on overdrive, and here I was, "Captain Brilliant", running on a whole lot of adrenaline and a lack of common sense, chasing what easily could have been a raging Bull Moose through a possible shooting zone. I think you can say brilliant! The lesson here is to know the season you are in, what that season means as far as hunting, and how an animal might be expected to react at that time of year. Of course, it is never good to run after an animal no matter what the season. Brains over bravado, as only fools rush into the woods after a moose no matter what time of year it is. No more moose marathons for me.

It is so easy, when out on a trail, to get caught up in what is immediately around you, that you forget to look around at everything else that you should be taking into consideration. I think most of the time this is harmless, but none the less, you should truly take the time to look up, down, and all around you. And take in everything from time to time. If you don't, then sometimes you may stumble into a situation that isn't exactly what you want it to be; one that could be unsafe, and one that could have been avoided. Do you get the feeling I might have learned this lesson the hard way again? You would be one hundred percent correct to think that, and I found out the hard way that your surroundings include more than what is directly in front of you. I guess one way to think of it is, with your head down you see a little, and with your head up you see a lot. Tunnel vision causes a narrow focus and that leads to being unaware of the entire world around you. Many creatures move quietly. Sometimes they may not be moving much at all and you are the one moving into their surroundings. Animals are not always great at knowing what is around them either. I have found this to be true several times and this was one of those times.

I was walking along a trail, going through meadows that were filled with butterflies, insects, and flowers. I was checking out all these natural pollinators and snapping away with my camera as I went on. The field of flowers gradually morphed into an area of blueberry bushes. I was checking out the crop on the first few plants when I heard a crack in front of me. I looked up and there was a bear looking right back at me. It was quite clear neither of us had seen the other because we were both busy doing our own thing. This is an easy way to get yourself into a bad situation, as startling any wild animal can cause it to go into fight mode out of self-preservation; fight or flight. Sometimes you get lucky and they just look at you kind of dumb founded like this one did. I am sure I had a dumb founded look on my face as well.

The situation could have been worse. The bear could have had young with it or near it. By not being aware of your surroundings, you could easily put yourself between the two and that changes the equation again and most definitely not in your favor. Any animal or bird is much more likely to attack or charge if you are between it and its young. It doesn't matter if you mean harm or not. All the animal or bird knows is that you are near what it covets most in this life: its young.

The best thing you can do is to slowly back away. Do not make eye contact with the animal and do not turn your back on it till you have put some substantial distance between you and the animal. DO NOT RUN and do not make sudden movements. You want to remove yourself quickly and quietly while letting the animal get back to doing whatever it was doing before. It may even leave when you do, but before heading back up the trail make sure you wait awhile as it could have moved just out of sight and a second encounter would not be a good thing for either of you.

As I have stated before, please read up and talk to professionals like a ranger or warden about how you should react in these situations. Please, for your own personal safety, make sure you are aware of your surroundings and enjoy what is close and what is far. Looking up every now and then could get you a glimpse of something magnificent that you would not see by keeping your head down. It may also give you the ability to observe something like a bear without intruding on it. So enjoy nature to its fullest with a wide view.

I could write other stories of my mistakes or mishaps in the wild but you will soon have some of your own. Just don't be a fool and rush in without giving yourself the best chance possible for success and fun. Think ahead and plan ahead for what may be, and do not take chances. It will all be there another day. You need to be there to see it for all the days to come. Just remember fools rush in.........

Long Lens Couldn't Keep Me Away

I am often out all times of the day and have learned that, despite what books often say, wildlife doesn't go by the book. They are out when they need to be out and moving when they feel they need to move. I think this is often a result of different pressures they face in their environment. Things such as food, humans, predators, and other things seem to play into when they are out. So they tend to go by their own needs and own clock.

They do other things that often do not make sense and have no easy explanation. It could be as simple as a sense they have that we do not know about or understand. In that case, we would likely cast it off as odd behavior or maybe as an animal that just isn't too bright. It could be attributed to many things, but are we just looking to assign logic to what seems illogical?

I was out at mid-day, walking along some power lines during hunting season last year. I kept seeing fresh deer tracks and occasionally a deer would pop up out of the woods and across the trail ahead of me. Since the camera was hanging from my shoulder, I didn't even try to get a shot, but just enjoyed the pleasant surprises. I do not know if I would have been able to get a shot even if I tried, considering how unpredictable their jumping out was as I walked along.

As the day went on, I had found numerous birds, flowers, and insects to photograph and was very satisfied as I made my way back through the trail I had passed over earlier in the day. I certainly wondered whether or not I would see deer again as the sun was setting low on the horizon. I heard distant gun fire and figured that would take care of that, the deer would definitely stay in the woods now. I picked up my pace a bit for I was anxious to be out of the woods too, and I would have to trek through a patch of woods to get from the power lines to the car.

As I crested a hill, I had a feeling that I should stop right where I was for a few minutes. I stood and all was silent. It seems like everything around you stops and listens to you after you stop moving or making noise. Many forest creatures interpret you as a threat and in truth, to many of the wildlife out there we are a threat. History has proven it true time and again for we humans have had a hand in the extinction or near extinction of many species.

When you are traveling on a trail and you wish to see or hear wildlife, I have found it essential to stop every so often and just stay still. After 10-15 minutes everything will be as it was before you stopped there and nature will return to its normal rhythm.

I heard sounds from down the hill, off to the side of the trail, and was positive it was a deer so I got my 100-400mm lens ready and set the camera up. The birds around me were singing and darting past me but I was focused on the noises down the trail. As I listened, I was convinced it would emerge from the woods and onto the trail. I stood tall and braced the camera to keep it from shaking.

A good sized deer walked onto the trail and stopped in the middle of it. He looked around and sniffed the air. I knew he could smell me as the wind was coming from behind me. The deer looked up the hill straight at me. I snapped a couple of shots off which caught the deer's ears twitching as it zeroed in on the unfamiliar sound.

I expected it to turn and run for the woods. I was a human with a big object in my hands pointed in its direction and the object made noises too. I was truly baffled as it began to walk up the trail towards me. I stood and occasionally took pictures. It kept on coming and was now less than fifty yards away from me. I lowered the camera to just watch, as I was in shock that this was truly happening. The distance kept closing and I put the camera back up to my face and snapped more images. A noise to my right stopped the deer in its tracks, and

it propped its ears and tail up, focusing its attention in that direction. I lowered the camera and looked to where the deer was staring. Something was coming through the low shrubs right towards me. The deer sensed no danger and relaxed its ears and tail. I, on other hand, wasn't sure what to think of the noise. Something was slowly moving my way.

I looked back at the deer who was only ten yards away from me. Our eyes met and it shook its head and snorted at me. I snorted back. I generally will mimic animals or birds when they are close enough and make a noise.

The deer turned and walked back down the trail. It was almost as if it came up and was letting me know it knew that no matter how big my lens was that I couldn't scare it away.

The noise next to me was getting very close. I wasn't sure if it was a ground hog, mink, weasel, fox, porcupine, opossum, or a skunk, but I was going to try and get a shot of it. I switched to a smaller lens and backed up a little bit. Then I lay down directly across from where I was anticipating that whatever it was would be coming out of the brush.

I was anxious about the unknown creature but not afraid. Slowly a face pops out and I realize it is a porcupine. It heads straight towards my lens. Right about this time I am

hoping that it truly is just an old wives tale that they can throw their quills. This would not be the way I wished to find out if they really could toss them as I am face to face with this porcupine. I utter a very soft and gentle "hello" and immediately the quills rise up all over its body. I tense as it turns sideways only feet from me. After a brief pause it moves past me as fast as a porcupine can and scrambles up a tree.

I slowly begin to breathe again and then get to my feet. I take a shot or two of it in the tree. I then look down the hill to see the deer has been joined by a few others. It has grown dim as the sunlight is fading fast. I smile and am thankful for these experiences and head off on the trail.

As I drive home, I try to figure out a logical reason for the deer walking up to me and simply can't think of one. Another encounter to be filed as inexplicable to me.

Your Safety

There is a lot going on in the woods that requires you to think ahead for your own safety and I hope that you already know the majority of this before ever heading into the woods or hiking up one of the mountains. It is always good to refresh yourself on the latest in safety and survival techniques. There are many resources for this which includes books written by professionals, courses, online bulletin boards, and even personal guides. It is also always wise to check the latest trail and weather conditions, which can often be found online. The information I offer you in this chapter is based on my years of personal experiences in the woods, combined with the use of many of the above resources. However, I am far from an expert so take this as additional information to consider and not any hard fast rule.

I always take the time to read up on trail conditions and one resource I often utilize is "Rocks On Top," which is a great trail report site online. Many hikers post updates of what is going on with each trail they have recently travelled. It covers things like blow downs and washouts and will also tell you if a trail is in great shape. The forums here are also a great place to ask questions. I always keep up on the weather reports, but take it with a grain of salt to be honest, as the weather in the mountains is fickle. I prepare for the worst case scenario and make sure I have appropriate gear should that worse case happen. I am frequently in the woods and on trails alone as it is the easiest way to discover wildlife. I generally hike trails during the weekdays to avoid the large crowds that utilize the trails on the weekends. I find it easier to see wildlife during the week when you can minimize your noise and not have to worry about the sounds being made by others. On the weekends, the large number of hikers tends to keep the wildlife stationary or drives them away from the trails making it harder, but not impossible, to see them.

The main thing is to prepare, and prepare well, for your trip. Do not count on cell phone reception. Bring a GPS unit with you but be prepared to have it go on the blink. It is always best to have a map and compass at your side. One of the things I also do is take a picture or put a colored tie at a junction so I know which way to go when I come back. Make sure to remove any colored ties or items you have set out when you leave. I believe it is important to take the time after passing a junction to turn around and see what it will look like coming back; this is when I take a picture if possible. I truly used to think that I would just know which way to go, and I did 99% of the time, but the one time I didn't, a six mile hike turned into a thirteen mile ordeal that left me feeling quite vulnerable. I finally got back to my car after dark without the benefit of a headlamp. It turned into a day with many lessons learned as I was under prepared. I realized things can and do go wrong out there, even for the most experienced hikers. So simply save yourself from some scared moments and potential danger by preparing from the start.

Hiking alone offers many challenges and can certainly increase the danger to the hiker as there is nobody there to help you should something go wrong. Counting on someone to happen along the trail, should difficulties arise, is not enough to keep you safe. Make sure someone knows your plan and stick to that plan. Deviating from a plan makes no sense, so don't do it. There are GPS and tracking units now available that can post your position to a website so others can follow along. SPOT is the one I use and have truly enjoyed it. This does not give you the ability to break from the plan you left behind for others. Any electrical device can malfunction at any time and should only be considered a convenience on your trips and not something to stake your safety or your life on.

Twice I have helped other hikers get off of mountains and down to safety. In both cases they were unprepared for the hike and had bit off more than they could chew. I do not blame either of them but there will not always be someone there to help you. In helping them, it changed my day for sure and left me wondering what would have to happen to me on the mountain before it would be too much for me to handle alone.

In the first case, a man was hiking up to Tuckerman's Ravine to see what the big deal was with people wanting to ski the ravine. On some weekends in spring, the number of people in the ravine can reach into the thousands and is quite the sight. Many people mistake the fact that, although thousands of people head up to the Ravine, that it is not a walk in the park to get there. You will earn your way there and in some cases the terrain is not friendly. Please learn not to take anything for granted and speak with others about the trails before assuming anything. This man assumed and he was wrong.

I met him just short of the Hermit Lake Shelters where he was stopped along the side of the trail, sitting on a rock.

Hermit Lake Shelters are roughly 2.4 miles up the trail and just below the bowl of the ravine. They offer a nice place to take a break before finishing the rest of the trip to the bowl or preparing to climb all the way to the summit of Mt. Washington. He was having trouble breathing and said he had fallen down a couple of times already and was feeling cold too. He was soaked from the water running down the trail on this spring day and was not prepared for the snow, slush, and ice that made up the base of the trail. The river of water only made it worse for all those going up and down the trail, as finding a solid place for each footstep was difficult.

He did not have the proper equipment for what he was trying to do and that almost always equals trouble in the mountains. He was dressed in a cotton t-shirt, blue jeans, and sneakers. He did not have water or snacks and had obviously not understood that, while 2.4 miles does not sound all that far, it truly is when you add in the conditions of the trail along with gaining 1,800 feet in altitude along the way. The trail is relentless and does not offer you flat sections to recover and catch your breath. You truly needed to stop and take breathers on this trail.

141

I offered him some of my water and a power bar which he reluctantly took from me. I could tell he was embarrassed and I told him not to worry as I had plenty and could get more water with my filter if I needed it. I stayed with him for fifteen minutes and he was still having a tough time breathing, so I suggested he head back down rather than up. He had asked if he was close and I said the shelter was no more than a third of a mile away, but the trip to the bowl from there was a steeper and more slippery climb than what he had already hiked. I said he also needed to consider the fact that he was cold already and he was not even in the open where the wind would be cold and strong, as it always seemed to be in the bowl regardless of how it was down in the valley. He said he would head down and we said our goodbyes but as he stood up, he staggered and I could tell he was in for a long trip down if he went alone. I was unsure how he would be and offered to go with him. He assured me it wasn't necessary but I told him it was just time to be realistic and that my help would make it much easier and would help pass the time as well. I took out a spare windbreaker from my backpack and handed it to him. He thanked me and then I handed him my hiking poles and explained that these would make it much easier for him and that my stabilizers would be sufficient for me to get down the mountain. He looked unsure but I insisted and soon we were on our way, making slow progress, back down towards the AMC center in Pinkham Notch.

The going was slow, we took many breaks, and eventually we made it. I think he was quite relieved to finally be off the trail. He gave me back the jacket and poles with a warm smile. He said thank you and I headed off towards my car. He asked why I wasn't going back up the trail and I smiled before telling him the mountain would be there another day. It had taken enough from me on that day. I think he learned a lesson that day, and, while I will likely never know if he did, I know I did. And I certainly hope you did as well. The mountains can quickly humble you and you can consider yourself lucky if that is all it does to you when you make a mistake.

The next incident was one that I found to be shocking in many ways. It was a true eye opener for me in what can happen on a mountain and that you can truly not count on anyone but yourself out there. So be ready for it.

I was hiking up Mt. Eisenhower, which is part of the Presidential Range of New Hampshire's White Mountains. It is a 4,780 foot mountain and going up via Edmunds Path is about a 3.3 mile hike. I was about two miles into the hike when I came across a woman who was probably in her early sixties sitting on a stump taking a break. I stopped and took up a stump of my own for a much needed breather. It is always nice to chit chat a little with fellow hikers. It gives you a chance to hear about an adventure or maybe tell one of your own. I can honestly say that 99.9% of the people I have met while hiking are in a good mood and in a peaceful state of mind. In general, you just don't go out and head up a mountain if you are not interested in the outdoors. This means you run into people who are happy to be where they are despite the challenges of getting to the summit. The woman was huffing a bit, but that certainly isn't something that is unexpected as all of us hikers do that, some more than others. She smiled and said she was beaten by her adventure. I tried to be encouraging by letting her know she had already done most of the mountain and there were still a few hours of daylight left to hit the summit and be back out before darkness came. She smiled a gentle smile and said she wasn't going up but was headed down. I started to congratulate her but she put up her hand to stop me from talking. I looked and listened for the next few minutes as she explained her situation which changed everything.

She was coming down but not from summiting Mt. Eisenhower or any of the other mountains that surrounded us. She was coming down from Mt. Washington with plans on heading over to Mt. Pierce, then taking Crawford Path down to the Highland Center where she would meet up with her husband for supper. She explained he wasn't into hiking and was also recovering from a double knee replacement. Earlier he had driven her to the top of Mt. Washington where they enjoyed the view together before she began her adventure for the day. She had hiked all 48 of New Hampshire's four thousand foot mountains some twenty plus years ago and figured she could probably still handle doing something as simple as coming down from Mt. Washington to the Highland Center.

She admitted to over estimating her own ability all these years later and under estimating how tough descending was on the body and especially the knees. I personally have always found ascending to be a battle of proper pacing and struggling with your own self doubts as you become fatigued. Descending is a battle against the mountain and your body, in that your body takes a pounding with each step. It is very hard on the knees, ankles, thighs, and lower back as you come back down. Her body was sore and she was only getting worse with each movement.

As we spoke, we were passed by a young man on a mission who smiled and said hello, but kept on trucking up towards the summit. Then a family of four passed us with children in the age range of ten or twelve, on their way to the top. The parents smiled and one child asked how much further it was to the top, to which I gave the standard hiker reply of not far and to keep at it. You always offered not far and encouragement rather than discouragement unless the person was clearly not prepared. People will decide on their own to turn around and you do not wish to spoil the hike for them by saying you have such-n-such left to still go through.

I asked the woman if she had a cell phone to call her husband from the parking lot at the start of Edmunds Path. She did not, and he did not have a cell phone anyway. I had a cell phone and also the numbers for local ranger stations and the AMC Visitor Centers in the region but there was no cell service on the trail. I asked if she needed my help and she said she could make it on her own by taking it slow and stopping often. She had plenty of water and snacks too. So I told her I would summit and if I met her on my way back down then I would walk out with her. She smiled and thanked me.

I looked back a few times until I couldn't see her sitting on the stump any longer. I battled with myself about leaving her but there was nothing I could do except walk and stop with her down the trail. I figured she would be down and gone by the time I made it back to the lot. Undoubtedly someone else would walk with her down the trail to the parking lot and give her a ride over to the Highland Center to meet her husband. I knew the lot had quite a few cars in it, so there should be at least ten others on the trail as it was the only trail accessible from that lot.

I refocused and battled my way up to the summit. I passed three others hikers on the way up who were headed down. I mentioned a lady they may want to check on and continued. Soon I was on the summit with a few others, including the young man on a mission and the family. In fact, I took pictures for the family before they left the summit. I mentioned the woman and they said they would make sure to check on her. I sat and took in the splendid view while enjoying some food. I sat and rested but inside I had a feeling I should be heading down the trail, not sitting here. I learned long ago to listen to those thoughts or intuitions. I packed up and headed for the trail.

I hustled down the trail as fast as I safely could scurry without risking a fall or a slip. A simple fall can suddenly make getting off of the mountain and out of the woods a very difficult task. So if you're going to push it, then try to keep it within limits, as you will be no good to anyone else if you get injured. Instead of being the one to help someone, you will turn into someone in need of help.

I was making good time and soon I saw her sitting on a stump. She looked up and gave me a weary smile. She had not moved very far at all despite the time that had passed. It had probably been an hour and a half since I had left her and yet she had moved maybe a half mile. I was worried as it didn't take much to figure out she was not going to make it to the Highland Center and she would be hard pressed to make it down to the parking lot before dark.

I sat down, caught my breath, and had a snack. I looked at her and asked how she was doing, to which she replied not very well. Her body ached and her feet were quite swollen. I could see her ankles were probably double what they should have been and that undoubtedly meant her feet were not fitting well in her boots. She truly looked worn out and even a little scared.

I told her I would stay with her and help her out but we had to try to keep moving; that it would get dark soon and her husband would begin to worry and so would the people expecting to hear from me. She tried to convince me to go on alone and that she would be just fine. I told her that simply was not going to happen and I would not leave her alone. I asked about the others who had passed and she said they said hello but that was about it. While it may be uncomfortable to ask if someone needs help, or it may just not be your personality to do so, if you sense someone is struggling, it is important to at least stop and try to get some information from them and assess how they are. Some people are just so afraid to help or be delayed or inconvenienced, that they just move on. To me, it is about what I would want done for me and the fact I just couldn't sleep at night not knowing how it turned out. I like to sleep well.

So, on we went as she slowly took each painful step until she just needed to stop again. I could see she was only going to keep getting worse but she was a trooper and we battled on a few more times. I had taken her pack but that didn't seem to help either. The swollen legs from toes to hips were just going to keep her moving slow. She kept telling me to go onward without her. I said I just couldn't do that.

During our next break, I asked if she thought she needed a ranger or someone to help get her down, but she reassured me she could eventually get there on her own. I told her that I was starting to wonder and thought we should come up with a plan as it was getting dark now. So we tossed out a few ideas and, in the end, we agreed that I would run down the mountain and leave her behind with water and snacks. I would get to the parking lot and call the Highland Center to reach her husband to say where she was and then let the Rangers know the situation as well. Then I would call the people expecting to hear from me to give them an update. I would then need to hike back up to her and finish helping her to get off the mountain.

Off I went and I kept trying to keep myself calm while walking at a safe pace. It seemed like forever but I made it to the lot and made the call to her husband via the Highland Center. He asked me to wait for him at the parking lot before calling the Rangers. I waited despite my reservations.

He pulled into the lot, and as he climbed from his car, it was clear he would not be able to go on the trail himself as he was still using crutches from his recent surgery. I explained that she was tired and sore but in good spirits. I figured it would be another hour before she was here at the parking lot at best. He said as long as she could move then he didn't think the Rangers were needed. I disagreed with him, but it was his wife and decided it was his call to make, so I headed back up the trail to find her.

In about thirty minutes I found her shuffling along. She was in continued motion now at least and I asked if she had gotten a second wind. She smiled and said it was called fear of being in the dark woods alone. I smiled and said I understood that very well. Everything changes when you can't see around you and every noise seems amplified.

151

We were making progress and she seemed to have found even more energy knowing her husband was ok and waiting in the lot. Finally, when we were about fifteen minutes from the lot, I saw a flashlight and as we got closer her husband was calling to her. Tears welled in her eyes and I heard a dog barking as it ran towards us. Her tears broke loose when the dog reached us. Her emotions that she had held in check all day were coming through now. Her husband was almost here now, somehow making his way through the narrow trail on crutches.

I tell her I am going to head off now since I know they will be fine. She thanks me, hugs me tight, and asks me to write my name and contact information as she wants to reward me for all that I did. I smile and say sure, knowing that I will not leave the information as this wasn't done for a reward but rather because it needed to be done for a fellow hiker in need. I would do it over and over again. I was thankful she would be safe. That was truly enough for me as I knew I would be able to sleep.

So please make sure to ready yourself before you go out hiking or exploring and be prepared for the worst. Do everything you can to help yourself, including not to be afraid to ask for help if you need it. Putting aside your pride is better than losing your life. Please keep yourself safe. Electronics can be very useful, but remember to not rely on them. Check the forums and ask questions. Read books or join a hiking group. Be safe and keep trekking in the beauty of nature.

Eye to Eye

The trip started on a cold, late January day with my friend Naomi. We had set out to visit Salisbury Beach State Park in Massachusetts. There were reports of some great birds that neither of us had seen, but the birds had been there for awhile. Such beauties as White-winged Crossbills and Snowy Owls were of particular interest to us. We were both very excited at the chance to see these birds.

As we approached the entrance to the park, there were a few cars stopped just a few hundred feet in and the people were walking around and looking up into the trees; always a good sign when you are looking for birds. So we stopped and, to our surprise, there were crossbills right there at the entrance. We walked and excitedly pointed to each one we saw, trying make sure neither of us missed even one of the truly beautiful birds.

The female with her greens and the male with its reds were right there before us and didn't seem to have a care that we were there with them. They went about their business: opening seeds and filling up. We giddily snapped pictures and tried to capture their beauty and behavior. I think we would have been happy to stay there with these birds all day, but we slowly retreated and moved on to see what else might be around.

As we traveled down the access road, we saw movement on the side of the road and stopped to see if we could figure out what it was. Snow Buntings, and a Lapsland Longspur was mixed amongst them on the side of the road. Wow, what an amazing find as a Lapsland Longspur is relatively rare for this area! So we bounced around trying to get shots, but the birds were not the type to sit still very long and kept jumping around.

Back to the car and onward to the snow-filled camping area. There were numerous cars here and there in the camping area, the occupants looking for birds as well. We walked to where the people were and realized, as we got closer, that the ground was covered with birds. Dozens and dozens of crossbills were feeding off the snow. We joined the group and began to photograph as well. These birds were not bothered by the presence of humans. Soon the flock of birds was literally crawling between my legs, and in fact, so close that I couldn't take a picture of them, as my lens would not focus. A truly amazing experience and everyone one of us was smiling widely. It was a special moment to be amongst the birds as if we were all just statues. Feeling accepted and not viewed as a threat, even though humans have now become a danger to many species. It was a throwback to times that no longer exist in many places, as wildlife is justifiably wary of humans. However, on this day, it was just pure joy throughout, as a crossbill would fly a short distance and land near you before hopping around and picking up morsels off the snow. Their crossed bills were so obvious and beautiful, as were the details and nuances of color in their feathers. Then an unknowledgeable human had to ruin the experience, driving past all of us, honking their horn in the hope of scaring the birds off, telling us we were too close to them. Someone who probably meant well, but didn't realize that the birds had

156

chosen how close to be, not us. After all, they had chosen to hop around between our legs. We had not walked up to them. That is always how the best experiences with wildlife are for me. They choose how near they want to be and what kind of experience we will have. I am just an observer. If I approach, it is always with their acceptance. It was time to move onward.

We made it to the end of the first part of the camping area where a boat launch was located. A few cars were parked there as well. From the car, we observed a few different ducks in the water that were drawing everyone's attention. We got out of the car and observed the birds along with the rest of the crowd. A Red-headed Duck, Green-winged Teal, Buffleheads, and a few others were swimming around and offering decent photo opportunities for everyone. A car approached and the driver rolled down the window, stating that a Snowy Owl was sitting over on a sand dune not far away. Everyone hurriedly piled into their cars and, of course, we followed.

It was quite obvious where the owl was, as the lot must have had twenty cars already parked with a caravan of ten more coming. Cameras large and small were being carried, as were spotting scopes the size of telescopes, and binoculars too.

We parked and headed toward the crowd. They had formed a fairly large circle around the sand dune. We both looked at each other and were in awe at the crowd and equipment around. Was this for a Snowy Owl or a rock star!?!

We looked for the owl but couldn't quickly pick it out on the dune. I asked the person next to me and I could tell they were surprised I could not see what was so obviously right there in front of me. Once I was able to figure out where they were pointing, it was almost as if the sea of dune grass parted and this majestic, haloed, white object slowly came into focus. It felt like slow motion to me as I realized I was looking at a real live Snowy Owl. The grass waved back and forth

revealing, and then hiding, the fire hydrant sized white bird. I looked at Naomi and again we both were doing all we could to contain the sheer joy of seeing the snowy. We watched and snapped as the owl slowly scanned the area for something to eat. It seemed oblivious to the crowd that was surrounding it. The circle was large and the distance we all kept was respectful of the great bird.

Gradually the crowd began to dwindle as the cold of the day seeped into your bones. It somehow managed to find its way through the bundles and layers we had on as it always does along the windy coast. Over time, there were just three of us left to enjoy the owl; Naomi, myself, and a man on the other side of the dune holding a very large lens, seemingly content to just stay and watch. The owl took a short flight and was now a little closer to us and more in the open. The other photographer moved around toward our side. Just as he was about to reach us, a salt and sand truck came into the lot to cover the icy ground. The owl didn't seem to appreciate the noise and flew away. We all watched as it flew silently with such beautiful grace. It landed about a hundred yards or so away over the dune. The other guy said he had enough of the cold and headed for his car. I looked at Naomi and knew that she was cold too, but would endure longer because this was such an awesome experience. I also knew she wouldn't mind if I went to find it at my own pace. So off I went....

I found a boardwalk that headed to the beach and it made the walking easier, but was quite noisy as the snow and ice crunched underfoot. I figured if the owl had flown close to the boardwalk, it would be gone for sure as soon as I was drawing near. I crested the dune and stopped in my tracks. There it was before me; no more than twenty yards away and looking right at me! I turned to make sure Naomi realized I had found it. She waved and I knew she would be on her way.

I knelt and then stretched out on the frozen boardwalk. The owl was watching me but was not interested in moving and did not show signs of being uncomfortable. It felt so strange to know it was looking at me, and, while I stole glances, I did not look at it eye to eye. Often that had seemed to be enough to spook birds. I crawled forward and was shaking as I did, but I do not know if it was the cold or just pure excitement. I stopped at the edge of the boardwalk and slowly moved my camera forward to take pictures.

Instead of just snapping away though, I felt this overwhelming feeling that I was supposed to look at the owl and not just take pictures. I fought with my fears of it flying away and slowly lifted my head till our eyes met. In that

 moment, I felt a deep connection with the Snowy Owl that seemed to throw a surge of power and being through my whole body. Our eyes were locked. There was nothing else in the world at that moment for either of us. It was as intense a feeling as I have ever had with an animal or a human being. A truly connected and spiritual moment of oneness with the owl which was a moment I would never forget.

I slowly began to take shots of the beautiful owl and it posed perfectly by turning its head this way and that. It froze and I could see through the lens something had caught its attention. It was focused, and its eyes changed from peace and calm to those of an intensity that I had never seen before. Moments later, I heard the calls of Snow Buntings and I knew the owl was going to go after them. The buntings kept flying our way and I knew our moment had passed. So I quickly changed the settings on the camera, knowing the Snowy Owl was going to pursue the Snow Buntings for lunch. It launched itself: its beautifully covered legs with sharp talons exposed, its wings unfolded to show a wide beautiful wingspan. Quickly it was up in the air and chasing the buntings. It was so truly majestic and yet so warily quiet. Not a sound, not even a swoosh of the air that is pushed away with its powerful wings. Off and out of sight so quickly.

I slowly got up and saw Naomi standing back a ways, and as I approached her, I knew she had done what she often has done and smiled before saying thank you. Naomi has come to know that some moments I have with wildlife just turn out to be truly special, and unselfishly she allows me to have those moments, rather than push forward and hope the wildlife will allow another's presence. I am truly thankful for her unselfish ways.

This was an experience of a lifetime. The Snowy Owl undoubtedly knew Naomi was on the boardwalk but it never flinched or looked towards the boardwalk behind me. Every time I think of the moment or tell the story, I can still see those golden eyes so very clearly and feel the touch they had on my soul.

Orange is a beautiful color!!

I had never really worn blaze orange and quite frankly didn't have the need for such a color. I suppose, back in the days during football practice, I may have had a bright color on to make sure nobody hit me; quarterbacks get protected if not pampered. Living in the city certainly kept me from needing to wear orange. Add to that not being a hunter, and you can understand why I lacked orange in my wardrobe. Blaze orange was not my thing until I started venturing into the woods to hike and photograph. All of that has since changed for the simple fact that I like to be alive.

We are told every fall as hunting "season" approaches to make sure that we are wearing blaze orange in the woods and that our pets should have it on as well. The pets even need it in their own backyards in many places these days as shootings of dogs and horses seem to be on the rise.

Most of us are pretty good about following those rules in November and most hunters are great about making sure they know what they are shooting at before pulling the trigger. However, there are exceptions to every rule and hunting "season" really never stops. We are not well advised of that fact.

A couple of specific incidents genuinely opened my eyes, scared the bejeebers out of me, and certainly placed me within the sights of guns. I can tell you it is one of the most terrifying things in this world to have a rifle pointed directly at you with a finger on the trigger.

The first time I ever experienced this was on a hike up the ski slopes of Shawnee Peak in the late fall during deer hunting season. I was hiking up the slopes with the intention of traversing the length of Pleasant Mountain. There was a chill in the air on that late fall morning as I started up the slope. I was well prepared with my GPS, camera, map, snacks, and plenty of water. I was wearing a blaze orange hat and shirt. I was looking forward to enjoying whatever the day held for me.

I started at a brisk pace and was making good progress. I noticed deer droppings all over the slope and they continued as I gained altitude. Deer were definitely here and I was hoping to stumble upon some to capture a few pictures. I stopped to look around thoroughly to try to figure out where they may choose to stay during the day. As I was scanning, I caught a glimpse of something shiny. I quickly cast it off as a reflection of something the ski area had stored over to the side during its non seasonal months. I had a feeling though, that something was watching me from above in the woods. This didn't set off any alarms as it is quite common for me to feel this and actually is part of my connection to animals and very helpful in finding them. So I just put my head down and headed upwards figuring I would see the animal soon.

As I continued upward, the feeling of being watched began to change and a fear started to well up from deep within me that I had rarely experienced. I have learned that these primal feelings that we can get in touch with should never be ignored. If you are walking down a city street or up a mountain, like I was on this day, and the feeling of unease or sense of danger comes, then you really need to listen to it as there are simply times our senses and intuition are greater than we are capable of understanding. Just trust those instincts and check things out.

I lifted my head, fully expecting to see an animal that I had inadvertently missed, and now was invading in its personal space. Sometimes animals are so well hidden it is easy to miss them and that is instinctually their plan... I have stumbled upon them in the strangest of hiding places, often right out in the open.

I quickly realized it was not an animal that I was seeing and my knees weakened as I was looking up the slope at a person in camouflage pointing a rifle directly at me. He was at least one hundred yards away and I could not see if his finger was on the trigger or not but the rifle was in firing position. I had no idea what to do and with my knees shaking, I froze in place. As I stood looking at him, he slowly lowered the rifle and disappeared back inside the tree line. This was not a place I had expected to encounter a hunter, but at the same time, I was wearing my beautiful blaze orange. I knew he could easily discern I was a human and not a deer. My fear eased and I decided that he knew I was there now and would be careful not to shoot in that direction. I figured he had walked off in search of a different spot.

I continued to slowly move up the mountain but now my head was up and I was paying much more attention to my surroundings. The peaceful, leisurely hike up the mountain had now turned into me wanting to just get up to the top and over to the other side safely. I thought about turning around but there was no need for that if the hunter was a responsible hunter. There was certainly room for both of us on Pleasant Mountain.

I saw movement in the area ahead where the hunter had disappeared and my first thought was that it was a deer, as that is so like the nature I encounter so often. It would make perfect sense in my experiences for a deer to appear and walk across the open space to the other side. I soon saw that it was not the deer but the hunter. He came to the edge of the woods and again raised the gun to his head with it pointed at me.

I did not stop this time but continued to move forward up the mountain. I was now only fifty yards from where he was and while I was uneasy I was also becoming angry. I wanted to yell but thought better of it. He lowered the rifle and headed back to a spot in the tree line. I had time to think things over as I headed in the direction where he went as I knew that I needed to speak to this guy and find out what was going on. I knew that I could not feel safe hiking the mountain without knowing what the issue was with this hunter, and yet there was fear of approaching an armed man who had twice pointed a rifle at me. The thoughts raced through my mind on how this could turn out and yet I felt I had no choice as I also did not want to walk down the mountain with a rifle pointed at me either. Onward I went right towards the tree line.

I was finally close enough to talk to the hunter and the time it had taken me to get there gave me time to calm down and reorganize my thoughts. I calmly asked him why he kept pointing his rifle at me as I was coming up the slope. He said he was trying to see what I was carrying and if I was with an agency or with the ski resort. He asked why I had all the camera equipment with me. "First things first," I said to him and told him it was not safe to be pointing a gun at anyone. I was wearing orange and he clearly knew I wasn't an animal. He said he never had his finger on the trigger and that he was just using the scope. I told him there was simply no way for anyone to know that and the fact of the matter was that pointing the gun at a human was not right. He apologized at that point and we had a decent discussion about where he was hunting and where I was going to make sure to avoid an accident later in the day. I finished the hike without ever seeing him again.

I think it is imperative for all of us to understand that wearing blaze orange is not only important but essential. However, it is far from the only thing that must be done to keep us safe during hunting season. Our own vigilance while in the woods is certainly a big part of it. We have a right to be in the woods and the hunters have a right to hunt. Together, we can all work on being safe. Hunters should not point a gun at other humans even if it is to scope. They can purchase and use binoculars to see what is around them if they just want to look around rather than using their scope.

Hunting "season" always seems to make one think of deer or moose or turkey and, basically, a fall season we need to worry about. I found out the hard way that hunting "season" in one form or another seems to go on year round. My lack of knowledge led to a truly frightening experience for me and one that had me nervous in the woods for awhile.

I was not far from my home and was out in the woods early in the morning. I set myself up under the low hanging boughs of a pine tree. I was wearing an all white suit and had dug into the snow to make a comfortable area to sit. It was also a spot that I could see well from, but one where I couldn't easily be seen by anything approaching. I set up a box that sounds like a rabbit squealing a bit further away from me to try and get coyote, bobcat or fox to come investigate. I had never tried this before so did not know how it would work.

It didn't take long before a crack to my right signaled something was coming into the area. There were more scuffles and cracks as whatever it was approached cautiously. I began to get my camera equipment ready with very slow and deliberate movements. I knew it was crucial to be quiet and not to have my movement detected by the approaching animal. I was getting excited.

As it continued to get close, I began to wonder what it could be that was coming as the noise just did not blend with anything I had heard before and was not making sense to me. I just figured the animals were hungry and less cautious. I looked for movement with excitement and tried not to fiddle around much. I shifted the camera and suddenly two hunters stepped into the space and raised their riffles to their shoulders and peered down the scope directly at me in my secret little spot. My heart jumped out of my chest and I tried to yell but I couldn't seem to get anything out. I knew they were waiting for just one more move from me in the tree before they let shots go. I was sure I was going to get shot and that people would read about the stupid fool who was hiding under a tree in all white. It was February though!! It wasn't hunting season so what was going on!

I gulped and then yelled "No, no, no!" as loud as I could until their guns lowered. Then I yelled "Coming out" until I was fully out in sight. My knees and hands were shaking uncontrollably so I just stood there afraid. They looked at me and walked towards me quickly. They asked if I was ok and told me I was very lucky to not have been shot. I simply shook my head and could not find my voice. Inside my head everything was going a mile a minute. They had me sit down and one went over to turn off my call box.

I finally found my voice and asked why they were out there with guns. I asked if I stumbled onto private property or something. They said it wasn't private property and they were out hunting for bobcat, coyote, and fox. I said I didn't think hunting season went past the fall and early winter. They laughed and said that was the problem with people who just go off "willy nilly" in the woods. They said something is always in season to be hunted and the public just doesn't know it. I said that was true but whose job is it to educate the public to wear orange or use caution during the whole year? I actually pointed out they were not wearing orange either. They said it wasn't about wearing orange so much as being careful with what you do and remaining visible as well as aware. They said they pointed the rifles as they had no clue what was under the tree, but they would never shoot before indentifying what it was first. It really didn't seem to slow down the pace of my still racing heart.

We parted ways and over the course of the days ahead the incident would replay in my mind over and over. I had decided blaze orange would be a great year round fashion statement. The general public should be better educated on what is being hunted and when. The use of orange should also be advocated for more than just during the moose and deer hunt. I feel lucky to have come out of that incident alive and believe it is only because the hunters were being 100% sure before they fired.

So please be cautious in the woods and remember it is quite possible a hunter may be out there too. Orange can't hurt and can keep you safer. There are only a few hunters who are irresponsible, but for all of our safety, it is best that we do our part and not trust that the person with the rifle is going to do theirs, as it only takes one mistaken hunter to make any journey your last.

I have since recovered from this incident and learned to make sure I do everything I can to enhance my own safety in the woods and I anticipate that you will do the same.

A Treat for You

I have experienced so many special encounters and I have shared a few of them here. The stories and adventures were something I could only share via words and pictures. This story can be replicated with much the same occurrences with one major exception: you can be the one trying to have your own journey.

There are wild birds that will take food from your hand and all you have to do is go to the right spot. They are not small birds either and they are not tame. In fact, they have learned what humans can mean for them…food! The Gray Jays have passed their knowledge down over generations and have spread to different spots in the White Mountains. All this is the result of one bird that trusted one human enough to take a treat from him and pass that knowledge to its offspring. It is quite amazing really that these birds, Gray Jays, have evolved over time to understand that if they prompt the hikers that often stop at a few different spots in the mountains, they will be able to get free, easy food.

The Gray Jays know there are certain spots where hikers often pause for a rest, but more importantly, for a snack. They

 fly in and perch themselves in sight and give inquisitive looks to the snacking hikers. You cannot help but feel their stare and ponder what they want from you. Slowly, they move closer and eventually you feel the obligation to toss them a crumb or two. They eagerly grab it and disappear to store it. They return a little closer. Those who know the legend of the Gray Jays get the real thrill: holding the snack in their hands so the jay will land on their hand to get the morsel of food. A very cool experience!

My experience with the jays has been nothing short of amazing. I have had many experiences, of which I will share two with you and then I will tell you where you can often find them so you may have your own encounter.

My first experience was one that came after a hike up the Webster Jackson Trail which I found to be quite strenuous and very tough on the knees. Once I crested the last part of the climb to reach the summit of Jackson, I needed to sit and rest. The plan of the day was Jackson-Webster summits and back down the same trail. As I pondered this, I broke open an energy bar and began to eat. A bird landed on the rock across from me and was staring at me. I looked back as it turned its head from side to side, seemingly waiting for me to say something or do something. I had not yet established or understood my connection with wildlife. I talked to the bird and was amused as it appeared to listen. It was beautiful and curious. I told it I needed my food because I had a long hike ahead of me. It seemed to understand as I pointed to the distant Mizpah Hut miles away. It flew off and I devoured my power bar before setting out on the hike.

I finally made it to Mizpah and took a long rest before heading down Crawford Path towards the Highland Center and, eventually, my car. As I approached the cut off on the path, I decided to stop and chat with a few hikers. Then, in flew a Gray Jay and they smiled. I said I had just seen one on Jackson and they asked if I had seen what they do for food. I said no and watched as one of them put some trail mix in his hand and extended it. The jay looked very closely at all of us and then the food before it flew to his hand! It gobbled up the mix and flew off. I smiled widely and could not believe what I had just seen. They explained the story of the Gray Jays waiting for hikers and free handouts. The bird didn't come back so I was not able to try it on that day. I was disappointed as I headed down the trail. I wanted to do this and decided I would try to learn more about it when I returned home.

It was simply fascinating to watch the bird come to his hand. This wasn't a pigeon or a gull, but a bird that lived up in the mountains. If you went to a place away from this area, the same species of bird wouldn't even come close to you. This phenomenon has only spread to a few locations since the first jay took food from a human. Gray Jays in other locales that are not part of these generations do not know that they can get food for free from humans because they have not been taught this lesson from their parents.

I did some research and found out about another hike where you could feed the jays. If you take Jefferson Notch Road to the parking lot at the top, you will be at the highest starting point of any hike in the White Mountains at 3009 feet, leaving only 2700 feet to the top via the Caps Ridge Trail. A tough and steep climb over the caps, with several false summits, awaits you if you make the trek to the summit of Mt. Jefferson. The good news, though, is that your hike to visit the Gray Jays is only a little over a mile ascent to the Kettle Rocks.

The "kettles" in the rocks were formed when the glaciers were receding. It is a great place to stop and relax before starting the tough climb to the top. It is also a nice spot for a picnic with the birds before heading back down. You can see a number of Boreal bird species on this trip as well, such as Black-backed Woodpeckers, Boreal Chickadees, thrush, warblers, and much more. But the main draw at the kettles is the jays visiting you.

The hike up to the kettles is easy in comparison to the hike to the summit, but do not be fooled. It is a demanding hike and you will earn every bit of ground to get there. The simple fact is that no hike up a mountain comes without effort. So be prepared.

I hiked my way to the kettles and settled in, waiting for the Gray Jays. It was not long before they appeared a short distance away. I took out a power bar and a bag of trail mix. I put some snack in my hand and held it out straight and stared at the jays in anticipation. I was so excited at the prospect of a bird on my hand. One flew right at me and my heart began to race. It landed in a bush about two feet from me, but would come no further. It just stared and seemed to ponder what to do next. I set the mix on the rock halfway between us and it immediately jumped down to pack it all into its mouth. It flew off and as I looked up there was another one waiting in the bush.

I held out my hand and again, expecting the result to be the same, but, after turning its head back and forth, it leapt towards me and onto my hand. It gobbled up the food, causing me to break into a smile from ear to ear. My jaw dropped in amazement because these birds are about the same size as the regular Blue

Jay that many of us see so often and I expected to feel some weight, but the bird was truly light as a feather. I was in sheer amazement and joy at the bird being in my hand and taking the food so fast, yet so delicately, that its beak was not touching my skin. It flew off and the other jay was already back, wanting more. My friend and I took turns taking pictures of each other feeding the birds. Then we heard a call from not far away and watched as one of the jays soared back to where it had came from. There were two young, first year birds happy to see their parents with food. The parents flew to the young, seemed to show them the food before swallowing it and then

they flew back to get more. In a few moments, the young birds flew in as well. This was clearly a set of parents handing down to the next generation, the legend of the Gray Jay.

They landed on the rock beside me and began a funny little dance and call. I laid food down for them and they eagerly

181

took it, but were still too shy to take from my hand or to land on my hand. It was such an amazing occurrence to be so close to the young as well as the adults. They were so entertaining, and of course, you could not forget the adults for they made sure you knew they were nearby and ready to come get their own share of snacks.

This was truly an amazing experience and one of the first I had with wildlife. The encounter opened my eyes to the possibilities that existed of being close with wildlife without disturbing nature's own ways. To be able to be a part of it and take something positive away, but also, to leave something positive behind. I continue to visit the Gray Jays.

There are places in the White Mountains to view these birds but many involve hiking up to the areas and thus you have to earn the delight. The places I am going to list are the ones I personally know of, but there may be others as new generations learn and move on to new territories.

1. The Kettle Rocks on Caps Ridge Trail in Jefferson Notch.
2. The cutoff on Crawford Path where you can either go to the summit or to the Mizpah Hut.

3. Mt. Jefferson and Mt. Webster which can be accessed via the Webster/Jackson trail.

4. Mud Pond in Jefferson, NH. This is a fully handicapped accessible trail, is only six tenths of a mile long, and the gray jays sometimes come to the platform at the end. They will take food, but I have not had them take it from my hand.

5. Route 16 around Cupsuptic Lake in Maine and the Boyscout Rd off of Route 16 in this area are spots to find Gray Jays as well in fall, winter, and spring.

Those are the only areas that I know. Enjoy the treat if you are able to, as it is not like anything else you will ever experience.

Epilogue

I would like to thank you for selecting and reading my book. I hope you enjoyed the journey and are now ready to start on your own. It is truly a mystical world out there and one that can take you on many rewarding adventures.

It is also one where you must remain vigilant and be prepared for the possible challenges you will face. So get ready and do not under estimate what your journey may hold. There are many resources out there for you to review. Use them to your advantage.

Enjoy all of Mother Nature's offerings, from the smallest to the largest, the obvious to the not so obvious. Again, thank you and take what is given...

To see more of Lloyd's Photography:

http://lloyd-alexander.artistwebsites.com/

Acknowledgements

There are so many people to thank for helping me get this project going and seeing it through to the end. Any project or undertaking such as this truly takes the support and encouragement of those around you to help you get past the tough spots.

With that said, there is no way this book would have been written without my right hand friend, and fellow photographer, Naomi Levesque. Naomi, thank you for everything you did and for putting up with me during the process of completing this project.

Thank you Peg Porell for the countless hours you put in editing the book. I truly appreciate your knowledge and ideas. The book would not be what it is without you.

Speaking of putting up with me.... Thank you to Michelle Alexander. Your support of my photography and my late nights of editing and writing are truly appreciated.

Thank you to the Gorham Grind, Carson Lynch, and his wonderful staff for affording me a great space to write, along with great coffee and treats to keep me going. Also, thanks again to Becky Sladen for introducing me to Carson and opening a door for me.

Thanks to Don and Peg Porell for being one of the first to step up with a belief in my photography at the very start. You helped a dream become reality.

Russ Yeaton and the boys at Bug Light: I would not be where I am today without you guys. Your belief in me as a person, and as a man, helped me come out of a shell and explore the world. The things we shared together were truly moments that will last forever. Never again will I see a fox, a skunk, and a groundhog all eat together. You guys are all my heroes.

Mom and Dad, thanks for believing in my photography and giving me the ability to believe I could make my own dreams come true.

Thanks to those who have helped me learn and gain knowledge of wildlife over the years: Eric Hynes, Casey Hynes, Doug Hitchcock, Chuck Holmer, Leslie Bergum, and David Govatski. Your sharing helped me to build a solid base to understand the world around me.

There are more and you certainly know who you are....I thank you all for your support!

This project would not have been possible without the support of the following donors who believed in this book, and my journey, enough to fund this project. I can't thank you enough for making my dream become reality. Thanks for your kindness.

Marilyn G., Dottie O., Dave E., Mary M., Russ Y., Mary B., VSA Publishing, Lynn L.,   Shirley P., Dawn G., Linda M., Sandra T., David G., Naomi L., Kiara C., Kay A., Peg & Don P., Kathy F., Joanne S., Betty W., Jim B., Linda L., Michelle B., Susan S., Mikki F., Michelle T., Lisa B., Ann Marie W., Michelle A., Christine G., Karen B., Don S., Pamela D.,

Made in the USA
Middletown, DE
28 May 2020